Finding My Way
in a Grace-Filled World

William L. Droel

ASSISTING CHRISTIANS TO ACT
PUBLICATIONS

Finding My Way in a Grace-Filled World
by William L. Droel

Edited by Gregory F. Augustine Pierce
Cover design by Tom A. Wright
Cover art "Portal" by M.P. Wiggins, TheSpiritsource.com
Typesetting by Desktop Edit Shop, Inc.

Published by   ACTA Publications
               Assisting Christians To Act
               5557 W. Howard Street
               Skokie, IL 60077-2621
               800-397-2282
               www.actapublications.com

A note on style: Lower case c is used on the word *church* to be inclusive. Upper case capital C is used to specify the institutional Church. This book will explain the distinction.

Library of Congress Catalog number: 2005922596
ISBN: 0-87946-285-X
Printed in the United States of America
Year 10 09 08 07 06 05
Printing 10 9 8 7 6 5 4 3 2 1

Contents

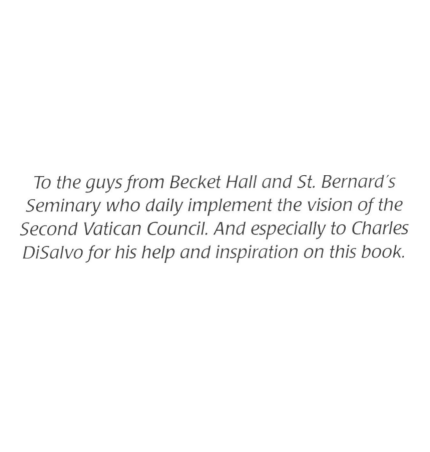

To the guys from Becket Hall and St. Bernard's Seminary who daily implement the vision of the Second Vatican Council. And especially to Charles DiSalvo for his help and inspiration on this book.

A Word from the Publisher

What can I say about my friend Bill Droel? First of all, he is one of the funniest people I know. Not in a "Ha, ha, have you heard the one about…" kind of way but in the way he shines a light on the silliness of how seriously we humans usually take ourselves. Nor does Bill exempt himself from this scrutiny, which is why he can get away with it.

Yet Bill is also serious, especially about the things that really matter most—like family, church, work and community. He is a "true believer" in the sense that if he says something he then feels compelled to act on it. You will see from this book what happens when you do that.

So when ACTA Publications decided to launch a new series of books called The American Catholic Experience, it was a no-brainer for me to ask Bill to write the story of discovering his vocation as a Catholic layman. *Finding My Way in a Grace-Filled World* is the worthy result.

In it, you will observe Bill's fierce commitment to the teachings of Vatican II, his palpable sense of place that has led him to put down roots on the south side of Chicago, and his unapologetic intellectual curiosity. Here is a lay Catholic who reads lots and lots of newspapers and magazines and books, even books about theology. What Catholic publisher wouldn't love a guy like that?

But Bill is not an armchair academic. He regularly takes his students from the college where he teaches to community events and on service projects. He oversees the Human Concerns Commission at the parish where he serves. He is involved in the daily lives of his two teenaged children. And he works hard to improve the lot of the homeless, immigrants and disadvantaged youth.

Along with Russ Barta and Ed Marciniak, Bill has been the driving force behind the National Center for the Laity (NCL) since its inception in the late 1970s. As the editor of the NCL's newsletter *Initiatives*, Bill has had an impact on both the Catholic church and the ecumenical and interfaith spirituality-of-work movement far beyond his immediate circle. I would insist that he has been a key voice in keeping alive the Vatican II understanding that the primary role of the laity is in and to the world, not in and to religious institutions.

So sit back and enjoy this unique little behind-the-scenes look at the vocation of a Catholic layman. Perhaps it will inspire you to reflect on your own vocation.

The American Catholic Experience books are all short, accessible, provocative reflections by individual Catholics on their personal experience of God and Christianity and church and life. Each is organized around a different theme, but the author is free to share his or her thoughts in whatever way seems to work. If you enjoy *Finding My Way in a Grace-Filled World*, I invite you to seek out the other titles in the series. You will receive "grace upon grace" (John 1:16) when you do.

> *Gregory F. Augustine Pierce*
> *President and Co-Publisher*
> *ACTA Publications*
> *Chicago, Illinois*

Introduction

I'd like to get rid of it sometimes—my vocation, that is. My vocation as a lay Catholic, which has taken many twists and turns over the years in New York, Minnesota, Rhode Island and Chicago, sometimes seems to conflict with what I'm trying to do.

But I can't let go of it. It is too strong, too compelling, too persistent. It places what I'm doing in a bigger dimension. It accompanies me, challenges me, and—when I slow down—it also comforts me. It is my vocation as a teacher, a journalist, a parish associate, a neighbor, a husband, and a father.

My vocation started approximately in fifth grade when I joined the altar boys at St. James Church in Irondequoit, New York. I first served Mass at 5:30 p.m. on February 11, 1959. The responsibility of serving Sunday or weekday Masses or wedding or funeral Masses fulfilled two of my basic needs: the need to belong and the need to make a difference. The altar boy experience also put me in close proximity to an exemplary pastor, Father Francis Feeney, a person who incorporated belonging and making a difference into his job and life style.

My vocation acquired specific themes during college, particularly the notion that a Catholic must be involved in justice or social change. I was surrounded by a great group of guys at St. John Fisher College in Pittsford, New York, and by many like-minded and compassionate women at Nazareth College, one mile to the east. We started volunteering in the migrant camps in Albion, New York. We eventually got very involved in the United Farm Workers movement. We also, after studying and debating the situation for perhaps too long a time, joined the Vietnam War protest.

My vocation became more serious and more fraught with practicalities when I moved to Chicago, Illinois, in 1978. There I married an Irish-Czech woman, Mary Ann Gallagher, from Mayor Richard Daley's neighborhood on the south side. Our teenage children are Chicago Catholics who attend public and private schools on Chicago's south side.

At several junctures, my vocation has meshed with the outward thrust of Vatican II (1962-1965), a watershed event in the history of the Church. In fact, Vatican II has been the one consistent, defining frame around all the twists and turns of my vocation. Whenever I get discouraged or lost along the way, I pray these words from Vatican II's *Pastoral Constitution on the Church in the Modern World* (*Gaudium et Spes*):

> The joys and the hopes, the grief and the anxieties of people today, especially those who are poor or in any way afflicted, these too are the joys and hopes, the grief and anxieties of the followers of Christ. Indeed, nothing genuinely human can fail to raise an echo in the hearts of Christians.

Then I say to myself: "Now, that's a mission worth giving my life to." In fact, the sixteen documents from Vatican II, enfleshed in a broad lay movement that I associate with the Council, say to me that we all belong to a community of faith and can make a difference in this world—on our jobs, in our neighborhoods, and with our families.

My vocation didn't come with a tour guide or a multicolored map. But I'm as sure that I have a vocation as I am sure of anything in life. It has sustained me over the years and propels me now to grow in faithfulness. I sincerely hope my children will find their vocations. As I say to them so often that they must roll their spiritual eyes at the words: "The worst kind of unemployment is to be without a vocation."

William L. Droel
Chicago, Illinois
Ash Wednesday
February 9, 2005

Disillusionment
as a Young Adult

The St. James parishioners, the Sisters of Mercy, the priests, and my parents all nurtured my faith through grade school. In high school and college I met more remarkable people who helped my faith grow. After graduate school, however, I was, as the euphemism goes, "away from the Church" for about six years. I went to Mass only occasionally. Several friends and acquaintances during that time were Church professionals, including some priests. But I was angry. The boyhood picture I had of Christianity did not match the reality of Catholic life I was observing.

The lifestyle of some priests and other Church employees caused some of my dissonance. The priests at my Catholic college and graduate school eloquently preached holiness to us, but more than one was having an affair. The priests taught dedication and missionary zeal, but some were lazy and others were fond of big cars.

Part of the dissonance was related to the Church at large and its moral teaching. Through the writings of Pope John XXIII and Pope Paul VI, I clearly heard the call for justice and peace. Yet some bishops in this country were ambivalent about the immorality of the Vietnam War. A prominent Catholic layman in our town, who owned a major supermarket chain, vehemently opposed the lettuce and grape boycott by the United Farm Workers and their supporters.

I was angry too because my own behavior did not match my ideals. In other words, I was a sinner—but at that stage in my life a sinner who thought perfection was the norm for anyone who professed to be a Christian. I lacked the capacity to forgive hypocritical bishops and business leaders. Rock bottom, I wasn't able to forgive myself.

After college I tried to be an idealist in a flawed world, often suspecting that I was instead a flawed idealist. I experimented with earning a living by working for social change organizations. My jobs were very worthwhile because they brought me into contact with several inspiring people associated with the war against poverty and with the peace movement, mostly in New York State but also in Minnesota, Rhode Island and Chicago. The experiment also took me deep inside myself. Although I wasn't always attending church at that time, I persisted in other spiritual disciplines: reading, examination of conscience, critical discussion with colleagues, and regular prayer. I used these things to stay in touch with my vocation, which I knew was the key to my happiness—if only I could make sense of it.

Fighting the war on poverty took a personal toll, however. I organized underpaid jewelry workers and hospital workers in Rhode Island. I organized for affordable housing in Buffalo. But I was always short of cash, my physical health was spotty, and my relationships—especially with women—were frayed. Stuck in idealistic gear, I was not rolling smoothly through life's normal compromises. Thus, by the late 1970s, my frustration and disappointment were getting the better of me. I either had to get focused and grounded or I was going to self-destruct in some way. To get grounded emotionally and spiritually, I reasoned, required getting grounded geographically. That's when I made the decision to move to Chicago, recalling a Rudyard Kipling saying: "I have struck a city—a real city. And they call it Chicago. Other places do not count."

I was further determined to ground myself in a specific Chicago neighborhood. And from what I knew about Chicago, committing to a neighborhood was also implicitly committing to a parish. The two entities are inseparable in the Windy City; therefore, my fascination with neighborhood became the path that brought my vocation back into full relationship with the Church.

The Sacrament of Neighborhood

There's a saying in my city: People do not live in Chicago; they live in neighborhoods. The saying is sometimes amended: Chicagoans do not live in neighborhoods; they live in parishes. In 1919, early in Chicago's history, eleven Catholic church spires could already be seen in the Back of the Yards neighborhood, an area of less than one square mile. Even today, real estate agents in Chicago commonly refer to some neighborhoods by using the name of the local parish, even with non-Catholic buyers and sellers. For example, a newspaper ad might list "a three-bedroom house in St. Ben's." In our local Burger King, I overheard a realtor say, "I just sold a two flat in Fives and a bungalow in Queens." She was referring, as anyone from Chicago would know, to Five Holy Martyrs parish and Queen of the Universe parish or possibly nearby Queen of Martyrs or, less likely, Queen of All Saints or even Queen of Angels.

In 1978, I drove my Ford Falcon west on Interstate 90 and rented a garden apartment in Chicago's southwest side. I could see two church steeples from the corner of my block. Buildings obscured the closest church, St. Clare of Montefalco, but it came into view and into my life when I walked around my neighborhood and under the church's threshold during my first weekend in what has become "home turf" to me.

The Augustinian Order had just assigned two younger priests to St. Clare's with instructions to get the parish up to speed, albeit belatedly, with Vatican II. This happy coincidence allowed me to experience the neighborhood as a primary source of grace, a conduit with God, a sacrament—properly understood.

Neighborhoods are not coordinates on a map. Organic neighborhoods, whose names, boundaries and identifying characteristics are fluid, can be defined as geographically-based support systems. Their intended purpose is to help people negotiate their way in the larger metropolis. Neighborhoods include libraries, restaurants, churches, clubs, and also people of every size, color, ethnicity, economic level, education, belief and occupation—or lack thereof. Thus the meaning of *neighborhood* transcends sidewalks and curbs, street signs and pavement.

> *Thus the meaning of* neighborhood *transcends sidewalks and curbs, street signs and pavement.*

I am interested in neighborhoods precisely because, as a Catholic, I believe my God is revealed through a community of people. As expressed by Father John Haughey, SJ: "The everyday noise of the city block is teeming with the word of God. The neighborhood invites us to partner with God in making the broken more whole." With that understanding, I have never regarded neighborhoods as merely a geographical phenomenon. My neighborhood is a sacred community.

My sensibility for neighborhood life comes from the dogma of the Incarnation, an aspect of Christianity particularly stressed within Catholicism. The circumstances of the Bethlehem event remind us that our extraordinary God is revealed in the ordinary physical stuff of life. The Catholic imagination is able to see Christ around the neighborhood in the same way he once was found in Joseph's carpenter shop and on the streets of Nazareth. The Incarnation means that everyone and everything is a potential sacrament, a source of grace "to those who have eyes to see and ears to hear."

Of course, like other sacraments, the neighborhood both reveals and disguises what it contains. God isn't somehow gloriously reigning from a throne at the end of my block or even seated in a reclining chair over on Garfield Boulevard. It takes faith to see God in the neighborhood, and that's easier in some neighborhoods than it is in others.

My Neighborhood
Is My Parish

For urban Catholics with an analogical sensibility, a parish is an extension of the Christian life celebrated inside the sanctuary. For us, the neighborhood is properly regarded as an extension of the parish. Thus my Catholic imagination is capable of feeling everything within the neighborhood as sacred space. Shops, homes, apartment buildings, union halls, ethnic clubs, and even taverns are all part of the link between parish and neighborhood. In fact, the equivalence of the parish and its neighborhood is taken for granted in some interpretations of Catholic doctrine, diocesan policies, and parish guidelines. A Catholic pastor, for example, frequently serves as the chaplain (officially or unofficially) to any school, shelter, union hall, or civic association within his boundaries. Likewise, parish facilities are by Canon law available to responsible groups in the neighborhood—provided there is no conflict with a parish function. This link between the parish and the neighborhood (a link made by many mosques, synagogues and congregations as well) goes a long way in humanizing a city and making its citizens more familiar to one another.

This is not abstract philosophy for me. Every day I walk up and down city blocks for a half hour or more—sometimes in my Marquette

Park neighborhood, sometimes in the Mount Greenwood neighborhood, sometimes somewhere I've never been before. This habit serves to control my diabetes, but it also puts me in touch with God through the faces, signs and buildings I see along the way. In fidelity to my particular calling, the spiritual life means paying strict attention to my surroundings, not fleeing them either literally or psychologically.

To be honest, however, I must disclose that my teenage daughter and I are involved these days at Sacred Heart, a suburban church about eight miles from our home. Our decision parallels the curious practice among today's Catholics of not being slaves to geographic boundaries. One parish bulletin, for example, boasts: "The majority of people who come here do so from all across the diocese and participate in different ways." At another urban parish the annual report notes that ninety-nine percent of the worshippers live one mile or more from the church building. A chairman of a *pastoral* council (note, not *parish* council) in the city recently introduced himself to me by saying he lives six miles away from the church building. This is an astounding statement for a Catholic in Chicago. In 1903, Archbishop James Quigley set down the goal of one parish per square mile in our city. By 1910, there was already a one-square-mile neighborhood on the southwest side with ten Catholic parishes and another nearby, only slightly larger, with fourteen parishes.

Today, literature and signs in many parishes in Chicago prefer the words *church, faith community*, and even *congregation* rather than *parish*.

The trend to think about parish life in nongeographic (Protestant) terms has advantages. It enables me and other Catholics to shop for enriching worship and thereby motivates some pastoral teams to improve their preaching, music and hospitality to attract the "liturgical shoppers." It also allows parishes to recruit talent and money from outside normal boundaries. It keeps some Catholic schools open by enrolling commuter students. It sustains some ethnic customs or clubs by allowing former parishioners, perhaps now living in a suburb, to attend functions in their "home" parishes.

On the other hand, nongeographic Catholicism potentially undermines something very distinct and valuable: a sacramental imagination attuned to street-level surroundings and an experience of community based on real turf.

From 1978 through 1998, I worshipped every week at St. Clare of Montefalco, at first only three blocks from my apartment. By coincidence my wife's extended family has been active at St. Clare since 1918, although she was not a parishioner there until we married. After the wedding we moved twice, each time about eight blocks from St. Clare. Remember, in Chicago eight blocks means there are two other Catholic churches between our home and St. Clare. Still, we worshipped there each week until the late 1990s, when we started shopping for a liturgy more vibrant than the one then occurring at St. Clare. By 1998, we were splitting our worship between St. Clare (one week per month) and a black parish (three weeks per month), even though the black parish is over four miles from our home. Then in spring 2001, I took a part-time job as a pastoral associate at—can an urbanphile like me admit it?—a suburban parish across the street from the college where I have taught for twenty-five years. So, with my daughter, I now usually worship at this suburban parish, Sacred Heart. My wife and son most often worship at St. Clare, where new leadership is reviving the catechism program, the neighborhood outreach, and even the liturgy to some extent. This quasi-geographic and split-family Catholicism, however, does not feel right to any of the four of us, but we also believe that worship is more than walking down the block to fulfill an obligation. So we struggle to remain faithful to both our values and our individual spiritual needs.

> *We struggle to remain faithful to both our values and our individual spiritual needs.*

Gaining Confidence from Parochialism

Despite my ambivalence about St. Clare, I still believe that the Catholic sacrament of neighborhood, with its parishes and parochial schools, makes a mostly unheralded contribution to the social fabric of our country. Far from fostering exclusivity and narrowness, the Catholic "ghetto" has assisted most of its people in becoming open-minded, racially tolerant, culturally assimilated, and socially sophisticated. Evidence suggests that Catholic immigrants successfully assimilate because they are launched from the safe harbor of their ethnic parish. Apart from any of its outreach programs or its involvement in community organizations, a parish makes a unique contribution to the political and social health of our country "merely" by gathering people for worship and by conducting normal activities.

It is true that more than one parish on Chicago's south side, often under the leadership of its pastor, has tried to keep a neighborhood segregated. It is true that not long ago students from a south side Catholic school shouted vile racial and ethnic slurs at students from other schools. It is true that some unions, led by Catholics formed in a parish environment, have systematically kept people of an ethnic or racial group out of a trade or occupation. It is true that some Catholic realtors have practiced racial steering, some Catholic bankers and insurance brokers have condoned redlining, some Catholic public servants have not afforded full civil rights and human dignity to gays, women, blacks, Asian-Americans, Jewish-Americans, Arab-Americans, the elderly, the poor, immigrants—take your pick.

On the other hand, when it comes to voting, Catholics are more likely than the general population to back social policies that redistribute resources to the disadvantaged, to new arrivals, and to the poor. By every attitudinal survey, Catholics are more tolerant of others than the general population. The tolerance quotient increases for each year a Catholic spends in a Catholic school. While bigots do not usually get promoted in the workplace today, Catholics hold positions of power and leadership in government, the courts, business, education, health care, broadcasting, and all the professions. Catholics are well known for their involvement in labor unions, community organizations, civic causes, charitable endeavors, and civil rights campaigns. Some of the most talented artists, filmmakers, singers and poets in the country were educated in Catholic schools. Catholics (and the category includes the new arrivals from Mexico, the Philippines, Southeast Asia, and elsewhere) are now the best-educated and wealthiest Gentile denomination in the United States.

So yes, the particularity of the Catholic experience doesn't always form responsible citizens. In some cases it reinforces prejudice. But overwhelmingly the Catholic parish, by giving people a secure base, actually propels them into a wider arena and gives them the skills and confidence to extend opportunity to others.

Each parish/neighborhood is a mix of the City of God and the City of Man. The Catholic strategy is to bless the neighborhood (or the trade union or the political machine)—warts and all—and to encourage its potential.

There is a genius for me in parish/neighborhood life. This social phenomenon, somewhat unique to North America, provides local attachments and a safe harbor that forcefully launches Catholics into the mainstream without severing their compassionate roots. This remarkable North American liberation practice is repeated as each Catholic immigrant group makes its way to Texas, Colorado, California, New York, other points on the continent...and even to my Marquette Park neighborhood.

Drawing Inspiration from Tragedy

My parents were married in 1947 on the south side of Chicago but immediately moved to upstate New York. My three siblings and I were born and raised in Rochester.

For four days in July 1964, when I was about sixteen, some black residents of Rochester rioted—looting stores, burning things in the streets, shooting handguns. Four people were killed and 350 were injured before the National Guard restored order. Subsequent riots, including the August 1965 riot in the Watts neighborhood of Los Angeles, brought the issue of black poverty and rage into national consciousness.

Even in early summer of 1964, the entire city of Rochester, lulled by a humming economy, had been oblivious to racial issues. Eastman Kodak Corporation along with several specialty companies like Bausch & Lomb Optical, Stromberg-Carlson, and the Xerox Corporation provided good employment (mostly for whites) while supporting many cultural amenities. Not one politician, business leader, journalist or ordinary citizen could imagine antisocial behavior such as a riot. Oh, everyone probably knew enough to avoid one or another inner-city street on the way home after a Red Wings baseball game. But to think there was a ghetto seething with rage? Never in Rochester!

In the months following the riot, some Rochester church leaders, mostly Protestant, did something unexpected. They did not recruit volunteers to repair damaged buildings. They did not raise money to compensate victims of the riot. They did not ask their national judicatories to pay *reparations*, an idea espoused by black militants and their supporters at the time. They did not ask for a government program to address housing or other issues.

> *The outcome of those discussions was startling, controversial and ultimately very significant for our little city.*

Instead, the church leaders formed a discussion group to study the causes of the riot. They used the book *Crisis in Black and White* by Charles Silberman (Random House, 1964) as their starting point. The outcome of those discussions was startling, controversial and ultimately very significant for our little city. It also became a major influence in my life, even though I was still in high school at the time.

Racial harmony demands an end to all discrimination in housing, education, employment and citizenship, insisted Silberman. However, in addition to the struggle against outward forces, the poor must simultaneously overcome the "sense of powerlessness and impotence, the conviction that [someone else] controls everything." It is hypothetically possible, Silberman argued, for laws and even attitudes to eventually afford blacks access to all their civil rights. Blacks, however, would never fully participate in society and the economy until they moved beyond an apathy rooted in a powerless self-image.

The civil rights movement, led by the Southern Christian Leadership Conference and the Student Non-Violent Coordinating Committee, directly countered that apathy and powerlessness. In doing so, SCLC and SNCC differed from earlier civil rights efforts like the NAACP. Instead of turning first to the courts to overturn discriminatory practices, SCLC and SNCC mobilized large numbers of younger people to protest exclusionary laws and policies. The direct action in the new civil rights movement not only brought changes in municipal laws and school policies but also a change in social psychology.

Silberman concluded his book with a case study of The Woodlawn Organization, a project of Chicagoan Saul Alinsky and his Industrial Areas Foundation (IAF). Silberman was impressed with Alinsky's ability to help blacks in Chicago overcome the defeatism that breeds frustration and rage. Alinsky encouraged blacks to take "direct action on their own behalf." Alinsky's notion of assertiveness, however, stayed clear of what today is called "playing the race card." That posture, Alinsky believed, usually only reinforces the victim status. Without an inner transformation, too much posturing and sloganeering only disguises an inner feeling of powerlessness, he taught.

While certainly recognizing that Silberman was not the final word on race relations, the church leaders in Rochester were sufficiently impressed with his analysis. Thus they invited Alinsky and the IAF to help organize the blacks of Rochester into a community group (eventually called FIGHT) that could demand job training, crime prevention, educational opportunity and more from the power structure of the city.

The reaction to the church leaders' action was as startling as the riot itself. It seemed that everyone was vociferously against the idea. Every TV commentator, every newspaper writer, every politician in Rochester had a negative opinion about Alinsky.

The more people spoke against Alinsky and the church leaders, however, the more curious I became. One Saturday I went to the downtown library and got Alinsky's book *Reveille for Radicals* (Knopf, 1946). Later—during my freshman year at college—a Catholic priest, Father Jack Skvorak, took me to a FIGHT meeting, which was held in a black woman's home. Listening to workers, homemakers and parishioners talk about their struggle for justice, I got hooked on the idea that ordinary Christians could band together with others to humanize the world. That concept became central to my vocation.

Since about the fifth grade, I had suspected God was calling me to something. My home and parish environment contained just enough people with just enough vocabulary to make such a thing plausible to a little boy. But calling me to do what? Even through high school I did not need specifics. It was enough to supplement normal teenage activities with, for example, reading some biographies of saints and doing an occasional service project. I also accompanied my father to Mass most weekday evenings during high school—something not as unusual back then as it would be today.

In college, however, I needed more specificity and, frankly, more amplification if I was to respond to my calling. From Father Jack Skvorak, from his friend Father David Finks, who was well-known in urban ministry circles, and from the lay leaders of FIGHT and some other groups, I caught the main theme of my public vocation: Full-time Christians are obligated to change social policies and institutions; and with some patience and sophistication such change is possible. Even when I am discouraged or in other ways burdened, I have never since been able to discard this central belief of my vocation.

Arriving in Marquette Park

My story about moving to Chicago's Marquette Park neighborhood and the wider topic of race relations will provide an example for how a vocation like mine can unfold.

I moved to Chicago in my late twenties. At that time, enclaves for young adults could be found on the north side of the city, even though the gentrification movement hadn't really begun. I chose, however, to live on the south side precisely because I wanted a real taste of Chicago's racial and ethnic relations. While looking for an apartment, I picked up a magazine in a corner drugstore. Its feature article discussed the Marquette Park neighborhood, specifically Martin Luther King's tumultuous 1966 march there, the subsequent weekly marches by the white supremacist American Nazi Party with its headquarters at the south end of the park, and the arrival of a small number of Mexican-American, Arab-American, and black families into the neighborhood. With all that tension, the place sounded ideal for me!

During my grammar school and high school years, my family visited relatives in Chicago each summer. During college I likewise regularly visited Chicago, including a summer-long *urban plunge* experience. I was fascinated by the block-by-block resegregation pattern that I observed on the south side. (The term *resegregation* is perhaps unfamiliar. Trying to understand its dynamics became key in my evolving understanding of justice. It means understanding why, for example, a once segregated, all-white neighborhood has become a segregated, all-black neighborhood. Or it involves understanding why, after court orders to integrate, the once mostly white public schools in Chicago have instead become *resegregated*. Thus today only nine percent of Chicago public school students are non-Hispanic white.)

It seemed to me during my visits to Chicago's south side that shortly after one black family moved to a white block, that block would turn from all-white residents to all-black residents. Nothing would happen on the next block until the block to the east was entirely black; then the pattern would repeat itself as the next block to the west was sold to blacks. There were certainly segregated neighborhoods back in New York, but I had nowhere else experienced this block-by-block white flight and resegregation.

I've now lived for about thirty years in Marquette Park. As a subtheme to this part of my story, it is worth noting that designating names for Chicago neighborhoods is fickle business. Real estate interests, municipal agencies, foundations, government programs, cable companies, aldermen, schools, churches and more have an interest in drawing boundaries and assigning names. Also, many people have a reason to emphasize one neighborhood name over another name—sometimes to project an upscale image, other times to qualify for some federal program. And quite often there's a heavy dose of subjectivity in a neighborhood name. Because of their differing experiences, grandma says her block is in one neighborhood while her grandchildren insist it is in another. Marquette Park, then, is my umbrella name for a place that is also in whole or in part called Marquette Manor, Chicago Lawn, West Lawn, Gage Park, West Elsdon, and more. (To underscore the significance of Midway Airport's positive influence, I like to call my neighborhood *Midway East* instead of Marquette Park; but so far my label is not catching on.)

I first lived in a garden apartment near Western Avenue and then briefly in a two flat overlooking Marquette Park itself. A drug dealer, as it happened, owned the building. His respectable tenants were meant to deflect attention from his activities. When I caught on to the game, I fled with my wife and our baby to the first floor of another two flat— this time surrounded by Polish-American neighbors. When our second baby arrived, some sixteen years ago, we bought a bungalow on a nearby street that was a mix of everything. Now the block is almost all Mexican-American.

The community organization's diligence eventually helped lead to the 1977 Federal Community Reinvestment Act.

There were already two community organizations and a well-regarded development corporation in the neighborhood when I arrived. One of the community organizations is the total opposite of the American Nazi Party. It is integrated and progressive on urban issues. It never, however, won the affection of area Catholic pastors in a heavily Catholic neighborhood populated back then by Polish-Americans, Lithuanian-Americans, Irish-Americans and German-Americans and now by Mexican-Americans. Therefore, the effectiveness of this organization is limited. Maybe the organization is a little too independent or too ecumenical or too progressive for the majority of the residents.

The other community organization was founded by Catholic parishes and supported, in part, with dues from each parish. In 1973, it pressured banks and other financial institutions to disclose their deposit and lending data by zip code. This allowed the organization to document redlining or disinvestment, the practice of denying loans and mortgages in a select neighborhood while still accepting deposits from residents of that neighborhood. The community organization's diligence eventually helped lead to the 1977 Federal Community Reinvestment Act, which outlawed redlining. In similar manner, the organization lobbied the state of Illinois to enact and enforce antisolicitation laws, keeping realtors from undermining confidence in an area by stoking fears of racial change.

As I learned, however, laws alone do not overturn bad habits. In looking for my own home, I initially visited a realtor—a University of Notre Dame graduate—at his office on the west end of Marquette Park. His office featured a large picture of a prominent elected official, a white man. Because of some mix-up, however, my return appointment was in his office at the far eastern end of the area. Sure enough, there was a large picture of a well-known official, but this time a black man. The realtor's regular practice was to serve his black clients from the east office and show them easterly properties. White clients were greeted in the west office and not shown properties in so-called "changing areas" to the east. This subtle form of redlining makes integration very unlikely. (By the way, I changed realtors.)

I was attracted to the parish-based preservationist organization when I arrived in Marquette Park. Over the years, however, we parted ways. My moral quandary with the community organization, as perhaps belabored here, illustrates a recurring theme in my vocation. In grammar school, I assumed my call was to moral perfection. My parents, my pastor, my teachers, and other adults appeared perfectly wise and fair. Only grudgingly did I come to realize over the years that perfection is the enemy of the good. I now believe that compromise, for all its faults, must be affirmed in any meaningful vocation to marriage, to parenting, to citizenship, and to work. Thus for me, the call of God is transmitted through the world of compromise. At the same time, each compromise I make must stay within the purview of perfection, lest my hope be lost. In other words, for me each compromise must be prudently made for the sake of inching closer to a greater goal.

Making a Tough Call

L et's get back to my dilemma with the community organization in Marquette Park. Reasonable Christians can disagree about the best means for achieving integration or equality. For example, someone who opposes school busing is not necessarily anti-integration. What makes strategic sense in one place and time does not always fit elsewhere. A compromise on one day might preserve a relationship needed to make two steps forward the following day. Given the history of Chicago's south side, for example, integration is impossible if whites start fleeing the day a black family moves onto their block. So preserving the quality of life for current homeowners in Marquette Park was a laudable goal for the parish-based community organization. Such preservation, for example, meant we opposed two proposed public housing projects that would have been heavily populated by blacks. The opposition to those specific housing projects—at least in my mind initially—was not racist. It was an attempt to forestall city agencies from labeling the neighborhood as undesirable (because of the concentration of low-income residents), setting off disinvestments by banks, insurance companies, and other businesses—which was the pattern in a few other areas of the city.

However, the parish-based community organization, despite its notable accomplishments, periodically signaled that it was retaining whites in Marquette Park precisely by discouraging new black homeowners. If that were true, I knew, Marquette Park's residents were ultimately being fed despair by the community organization, not realistic hope. But was I right about the organization's true character? After all, eight pastors—including my own pastor and friend, Father Jim Friedel, OSA, who had marched with Dr. Martin Luther King in the 1960s—were supporting the organization with parish funds and with the Church's credibility.

> *"We encourage buffer zones to achieve integration," he said. "Two square blocks for whites, then two square blocks for blacks, then whites, and then blacks."*

Shortly after I first got involved, the organization's director asked me to accompany him to a conference in Buffalo, New York, where we gave a workshop on our efforts. I was shocked when the director pointed to the checkerboard tiles on the floor. "We encourage buffer zones to achieve integration," he said. "Two square blocks for whites, then two square blocks for blacks, then whites, and then blacks." His assertion wasn't accurate in my opinion. But the attitude he betrayed seemed little different from the attitude of realtors and bankers who practiced redlining and racial gerrymandering.

My distress over the community organization was gradually shared by more people. In 1982, for example, the organization cosponsored a "white ethnic convention." In a certain setting a "multiethnic" conference is quite appropriate. But in the context of the campaign of Harold Washington, who would become Chicago's first black mayor, the community organization was signaling that neighborhood preservation meant keeping blacks out of Marquette Park (and presumably out of the mayor's office).

Once Washington took office, the organization circulated a petition calling for "white ethnic" opposition to his administration. In March 1984, it issued a "Declaration of Neighborhood Independence," a document that the great Monsignor John Egan of the Archdiocese of

Chicago's Office of Human Relations judged to be "inappropriate, irresponsible and divisive...race-baiting." Two Marquette Park priests, Father Michael Adams and my own pastor, Father Jim Friedel, OSA, threatened to withdraw parish funding and support from the organization. It then stopped publishing the inflammatory "Declaration," but it kept adding names to the "white ethnic" petition.

Some months later, the community organization picketed an otherwise innocuous "Unity Picnic," held in Marquette Park. It was sponsored by an ad hoc, interracial church committee under the leadership of a well-intentioned, harmlessly naïve, young Catholic woman. But again, by picketing, the community organization was seeking opportunities to signal "whites only" were welcome in Marquette Park. To my mind, the community organization had become an impediment to integration and equality.

With a few pastors and several lay leaders and with the encouragement of Cardinal Joseph Bernardin, we started a new organization we called Project Acts. It was subsequently called the Southwest Cluster Project and is now the Southwest Organizing Project. It wasn't billed as a community organization as such, because we didn't want to lock horns with the long-standing, though now thoroughly objectionable, parish-based community organization. Further, not all the pastors were yet disturbed by the actions of their community organization—at least not disturbed enough.

Our new organization was not some far-out group that tried to import blacks into the neighborhood. In fact, I sometimes described our group's purpose as "affirmatively marketing our neighborhood to young homeowners—whites and others." People ignorant of the complexity of race relations on Chicago's south side even accused me of racism over that statement.

But the truth is this: Circling the wagons to keep white parishioners in Marquette Park just doesn't work. People move out for lots of reasons—a job transfer, a death in the family, health concerns, and more.

First, circling the wagons only creates an undertow of fear that drives people away faster. Second, interest by blacks in area homes will take care of itself. Of course, that presumes groups like Project Acts insist on no racial steering in the neighborhood and equal opportunity on mortgages and insurance. Our organization, in cooperation with other agencies, thus polices the real estate industry and is active in human-relations efforts.

But the crux of the matter, we think, is attracting new whites to a block once a black had bought on that block. After all, for over thirty years, segregation in the Chicago context meant no white ever moved to a block that already had a black resident.

To attract whites, and thus achieve integration, we take advantage of our neighborhood's proximity to an airport. We do not resist commercial development like some community groups (and as was my wont in younger days). We see expansion of Midway Airport as a source of jobs.

We also supported a new el line (Chicago's term for a *subway line*) to link Midway Airport to the Loop (Chicago's term for *downtown*). We did some research. Members of our committee walked around some Chicago neighborhoods near el stops. I did the same while visiting Buffalo, Brooklyn and Queens. Jim Capraro, my neighbor and a community development expert, called his contacts in other cities with subways. The results were mixed: Some neighborhoods along a subway line were in decline; others were booming. Capraro rightly concluded that the key would be an aggressive publicity campaign to show that because of the proposed el line our affordable bungalows would be an easy commute to jobs in the Loop and at an expanding near-south university/hospital complex. We called upon all our contacts at the university/hospital, in Loop businesses, and in Chicago's media to put our brochures and video in the hands of potential homebuyers.

We also launched several ecumenical and multiethnic prayer experiences, dinners, and discussion groups. We continually sponsor programs to welcome new arrivals and reconnect longtime residents.

It is interesting (and comforting) to me that the community organization that was objectionable to my values quietly went out of business some months after we launched Project Acts. Its accomplishments over the years had been important, but it failed to stem the out-migration of loyal parishioners and had become unaccountable to the best aspirations or hopes in the neighborhood. Like its counterparts elsewhere, it eventually was irrelevant to the changes in the city and its area.

Welcoming a New Culture

The Marquette Park neighborhood gets a mixed report today. A steady upswing on the economic front is paired with a decline in social capital—a phenomenon certainly not unique to Marquette Park.

By early 1996, a Chicago newspaper proclaimed Marquette Park "a red-hot area." Real estate agents and building contractors were trumpeting the Orange Line (the new el that connects Midway Airport to the Loop) as a key impetus for accelerating property values and a growing demand for housing. The rate of owner-occupied housing in Marquette Park exceeds 85 percent, indeed exceeds 95 percent in its northeast section. Even the once-ridiculed bungalow, a squat style of house found by the thousands in Marquette Park, is becoming chic, achieving national landmark status in 2004. Chic or not, the bungalow is very practical as owners add dormers and refurbish basements to accommodate their needs. In addition to the airport and its related services, some area industries, a bank, some stores, and several restaurants are expanding their operations. The area's diversity is actually a positive for prospective homeowners. A City of Chicago brochure, for example, promotes Marquette Park with lots of inter-racial and multiethnic photos. Other agencies—private and public—consistently do the same. While many whites for many reasons moved from Marquette Park, block-by-block white flight never occurred, and whites have, in fact, moved into the neighborhood after it was integrated.

Mexican-American homeowners by the hundreds are also moving to Marquette Park. This factor was not in anyone's playbook back in 1980, although our organization and other agencies are enthusiastically responding to the newest immigrants. The Mexican-Americans bring capital, restaurants, specialty stores, children, working-class family values, and much more to our neighborhood.

As the economic picture for Marquette Park is relatively bright, however, its social picture is blurred. The challenges today are at least as formidable as in the late 1970s and early 1980s. Education, for example, is now a major concern. The public school system has quickly expanded to accommodate the burgeoning child population. But can Mexican-Americans and others really mainstream by relying on the mostly segregated, often crowded, and notoriously poorly performing Chicago public schools? Can the alarmingly high dropout rate from school among Mexican-Americans and others be lowered?

Ironically, as our neighborhood is adding to its Catholic population, Catholic institutions that historically build social capital are now in trouble. Catholic schools—including three Catholic grammar schools and a high school—have already closed.

For decades the Augustinian order of religious men were a substantial and creative presence in Marquette Park. They staffed two parishes and a high school and maintained their regional headquarters here. They assigned some of their best priests to Marquette Park, challenging all of us to live the fullness of faith envisioned by Vatican II. But the Augustinian Midwest Province, like their Eastern Province, is now abandoning urban parishes. This too is ironic. "The call into cities was a result of the Order's foundation and a fact of its life from the very beginning," details historian Father Balbino Rano, OSA, in *Augustinian Origins, Charism and Spirituality* (Augustinian Press, 1994). Because the Augustinians and other Catholic groups can no longer maintain their ministry in Chicago neighborhoods, the terrain in places like Marquette Park becomes more precarious for immigrants to our cities.

Nonetheless, Marquette Park's Mexican-Americans, with their black, Arab-American, Lithuanian-American, Polish-American, and Irish-American neighbors, are steadfastly making a home in my neighborhood—turning bricks and mortar into a sacrament of relationships and proving that diversity is the yeast of vitality.

Coming of religious institutions

Alone in a Crowd

The summary of my years in Marquette Park introduces a paradox I have experienced about my social-change vocation. My personal vocation absolutely requires me to mesh with all kinds of people. To remain true to my vocation, however, I have repeatedly had to stand alone.

Looking back, I exhibited a definite strain of perfectionism during my vocation's early years. My early feeling of superiority, despite its harmfulness, partially accounts for the longevity of my vocation. There's a sustaining edge that comes with being judgmental. On the other hand, my perfectionism made specific commitments to programs and people more difficult. I would inevitably be disillusioned with each new job or relationship. After an initial burst of energy, I often lost enthusiasm.

Gradually, Marquette Park taught me to stick around by holding onto myself by exploiting both my strengths and my weaknesses. I learned to adapt my high-minded principles to the give-and-take of a specific neighborhood at a specific time in its history and politics. Marquette Park taught me to tone down my anxiety over loose ends and to tolerate ambiguity. (On an interview for a job in marketing, one of my students was asked if she could handle ambiguous situations that were neither black nor white. She replied: "Maybe yes; and maybe no.")

Marquette Park similarly taught me that often the right thing gets done for multiple motives. I had to learn not to react to every comment, not to fight every skirmish. For example, I once overheard a principal make a racially insensitive remark, although in a non-school setting. In my younger days, incensed by the comment, I would have campaigned for the principal's resignation, sure that I was the morally superior party. Treading prudently in Marquette Park, however, I sought wisdom from two confidants about this case. The principal and school leaders, we knew, generally supported our efforts in the neighborhood. The school itself was an anchor for many families. With misgivings, I decided that a public confrontation with the principal would distract people from our larger campaign for integration. I privately let the principal know my displeasure, and as it happened the principal took early retirement about a year after this incident. So the right thing to do in that case was to keep my mouth shut.

Today I continue to attend meetings in church basements and at our children's schools. I continue to march with my neighbors against opportunistic or careless banks or real estate businesses. I continue to volunteer at a neighborhood food pantry. I continue to expose my children and my students to the variety of religious and ethnic expressions in our area. I remain convinced that, just as I saw in Rochester many years ago, ordinary people banding together can humanize the world. That idea is the bedrock of my vocation, the way I respond to God through my Catholic faith.

The God Who Loves My World

My vocation propels me into the world—its give-and-take, its rough-and-tumble, its hustle-and-bustle. My vocation is to live Christianity in that world, with a strong mandate to help its institutions recover their original nurturing purpose and better conform to God's plan as revealed to us by Jesus Christ.

Looking back, my Christian vocation was always about social change. My piety in grammar school and in high school was intimately connected to the corporal works of mercy such as visiting the sick and attending funerals. I eagerly participated in little fundraisers for missionaries while learning about their efforts to build schools and improve sanitation in far away places. In college I experienced the interplay between liturgy, personal prayer, and social causes. The United Farm Workers movement, in which I was active, was quite liturgical. Picketing a supermarket was a prayer experience. The same was true in the civil rights movement and the peace movement. My Christian vocation encompassed my studies, my work, my friendships, my citizenship, and all my so-called *worldly pursuits*. My Christian life felt seamless, if not always tidy.

Yet my worldly vocation has conflicted with two trends in modern culture.

Those who promote the "secularization" thesis say that religion is a private matter, something that should not overtly manifest itself in one's daily work. Shorthand for this thesis is: "A wall of separation between church and state" or "Religion and politics should not mix." The secularization thesis is supported by the Reformation theme of individualized religion. Phrases that betray this theme include: "My religion is between God and me" or "My morality cannot be imposed upon someone else."

At the other extreme is the theocratic position. Its proponents want to ameliorate all insecure feelings and ambiguous situations by imposing an explicitly religious culture. The advocates of this position, however, disagree on whose expression of religion should take over.

In contrast to the secularists, my vocation, heavily influenced by Catholic philosophy, says that faith is a way of life that permeates daily activity. Further, Catholicism taught me that faith is a corporate affair and that worship, morality, salvation, revelation and inspiration are intrinsically communal or social.

In contrast to the theocrats, on the other hand, my vocation says that any modern expression of faith must comport with reason and must function in a pluralistic world. Thus my vocation is lived precisely in the ebb and flow of modern culture.

There has to be, of course, some unease between the Christian mission and any society. The world is not yet the way God would have things, what Jesus described as the "kingdom" or "reign" of God. The defects in modern culture, directly attributable to excesses in its philosophical assumptions about individualism and utilitarianism, are many: too casual an attitude about abortion, too many handguns, persistent poverty amid plenty, assertion of rights often without acceptance of responsibility, unaccountable corporate executives and public officials, a withering of mediating institutions, and much, much more.

Wariness about the world is not new to Christianity. Catholicism, I am aware, officially condemned modern philosophy from the time of the French Revolution (1789) until Vatican II (1962-1965). Yet I never sensed that Catholicism condemns the world wholesale. I never heard that Catholics were to do anything but love the world and confidently and competently enter into it wholeheartedly.

Like other students, I took courses in biology, history, literature and more at my Catholic high school. We also had a religion class each semester, and in senior year we read some Catholic philosophers. My high school, as well as my family and my childhood parish, stressed that Catholicism values research, science, an intelligent life, and good grades on each report card. In history and literature classes, we certainly discussed the limits of human ambition. But while not glossing over the Church's defensiveness in the Galileo affair, my parents and teachers made it clear to me that Catholicism applauds exploration; is immersed in social problems; supports the arts; wants its young people to study law, engineering (like my father), sociology, business, and medicine. Catholicism is always part and parcel of history—the good and the not so good.

My appreciation for the reciprocal relationship between Catholic faith and modern society has only grown over the years. I was once having a drink with John McDermott, a civil rights leader in Chicago. We were in a club overlooking Michigan Avenue, the "magnificent mile." Observing hundreds of people up and down the street, I remarked: "Our job is to bring Christ to the marketplace."

"No," McDermott replied. "Christ is already there. Our job is to help people experience the compassion of Christ and help institutions reflect his justice."

McDermott taught me a key lesson: I am not called to evangelize a godless society. I am called to immerse myself in society not only to, yes, preach the good news (using words, as St. Francis suggested, only if necessary) but also to hear and see the gospel as it is lived by parents, public officials, neighbors, technicians, painters, waiters, and others—including non-Christians who anonymously or only very implicitly know the gospel message. The window between faith and the world is open. The Holy Spirit blows both ways through the window frame.

Amor'.

Pessimistic Fundamentalists

My style of Christian vocation is not shared by everyone. Among other trends (self-absorbed individualism or unrestrained capitalism, for example), the fundamentalist movement directly contradicts my understanding of the relationship between faith and the world. Fundamentalism, historically associated with Protestantism, is now percolating within Catholicism and is a major force within Islam. I consider this development one of the most unfortunate I have observed in my lifetime.

This fundamentalist movement is a reaction to the real and perceived dangers of modernism or modernity. Fundamentalism is pessimistic about today's culture. It seeks to restore an imagined golden age by fixating upon some pious practices or by harping upon select doctrinal points or by emphasizing isolated passages from a sacred text. Fundamentalism is always self-righteous, sometimes strident, and almost never interested in ecumenical or interfaith dialogue.

For all the defects in modern culture, then, I find fundamentalism (which is not the same as evangelical Christianity) to be very wrong. It is wrong for strategic reasons. Fundamentalists might win a vague commitment from a presidential candidate. They might put an "objectionable" movie in the dustbin with a national boycott or drive up ratings for a "favorable" radio program. But longer term, fundamentalism accomplishes the opposite of what it intends. Because of its stridency and its association with violence, it makes religion less relevant to the world. Modernity, now on the scene for over 400 years, is not going away. On the other hand, the world is demonstrably open to change through dialogue, reasoning, experimentation and genuine politics. Therefore, the defects of modernity can be (and have been) overcome by people who prudently, seriously, persistently, optimistically and critically engage modern institutions—seeking to align them with the best aspirations of humankind and therefore with the will of God. Fundamentalism, because it lacks any sense of flexibility, can sound the alarm, but it can never make the world holy.

> *Fundamentalism by its very nature abets those few twisted people who violently lash out at modern institutions.*

Fundamentalism is also wrong for moral reasons. Because it is built on fear and resentment, fundamentalism always has the potential for violence. The fundamentalists I know have never damaged property, advocated suicide, beheaded anyone, or even considered hijacking an airplane and flying it into buildings occupied by innocent people. In fact, they abhor those acts, even when they are done in the name of their religion. Nonetheless, it seems to me that fundamentalism has an unavoidably violent underside. Fundamentalism by its very nature abets those few twisted people who violently lash out at modern institutions.

This, by the way, is the same lesson I learned in regard to race relations in Marquette Park. Fear-mongering movements actually produce the opposite of what they advertise. Thus the fundamentalist movement actually makes it harder for legitimate religion to influence our society. By playing to people's apprehensions, fundamentalism debases the goodness and courage exhibited by moderate religious leaders of all faiths.

Finally, fundamentalism is wrong for theological reasons. We Catholics believe that God has been revealed inside human history and is involved in current events. In fact, "the Word became flesh" just so we can be sure that God knows what we humans have to go through. For us, God is always encountered through a specific culture—commanding people to use their talents, ambitions, discoveries and institutions to further the divine plan on earth. Our faith is that God's unique self-revelation comes through the historic person of Jesus Christ—a crying baby in Bethlehem, a sweating carpenter in Nazareth, an agonizing criminal in Jerusalem. Jesus Christ is part of the human predicament in all times and in all places. He does not stand apart from the ebb and flow of modern advancements. Jesus is in the newsroom, the laboratory, the recording studio, the engineering firm, the legislature, the classroom, and anywhere else people use their minds and hands to make a living, to serve society, to care for family, to promote genius, to instruct the young, to entertain a crowd, to communicate wisdom, or to just marvel at their world. This is, admittedly, a balancing act to be in the world, but not of it; to appreciate the best in modernity without baptizing capitalism or socialism or individualism or consumerism or materialism; to firmly believe that science, reason and human experience are paths toward the unfolding of truth while constantly remembering that ultimate truth resides in a transcendent God who supercedes all human endeavor.

good words n.e. the presence of Jesus in everyday life

Fundamental Anti-Catholicism

The term *fundamentalism* first appeared in about 1910 to describe a movement that had been growing within Protestantism in the years after the Civil War. The so-called "fundamentals" of Christianity were named in a series of pamphlets published in 1920 by Lyman and Milton Stewart. The Stewarts and others were basically reacting against certain trends in modern science and especially to the social gospel movement, which was an attempt to make religion relevant to progressive forces in cities like Detroit, Chicago, Rochester and Boston.

The early twentieth-century fundamentalists, by contrast, believed that each individual must resist all accommodations to the modern world, especially to theories like evolution.

Fundamentalism, as first codified by the Stewarts, is inseparable from anti-Catholicism as I've experienced it over the years. In fact, says professor Eugene McCarraher of Villanova University, fundamentalism "remains the largest, most toxic reservoir of anti-Catholicism" in this country. Catholics, says fundamentalism, are next to the devil because we use the wrong Bible (only the King James version is correct); we misuse the Bible (doubting its inerrancy); we worship idols (Mary and the pope); we make common cause with other sinners, including Jews, Muslims, and all those in denominations or faiths that do not require a personal "reckoning of sins to Jesus" and "judgment according to just deserts."

For example, when a group of business and civic leaders sponsored a Saturday clean up in my neighborhood, teenagers were recruited from schools and churches. They were to be treated to pizza and refreshments late in the afternoon. At a planning meeting prior to the event, I was assigned to approach a couple of nearby fundamentalist churches for volunteers. One was a new congregation that seemed to be making an investment in the neighborhood. Its leaders were initially friendly when I stopped by.

"Will our teenagers work alongside Catholics?" one person asked me.

"Of course," I replied.

"We can't participate then," she said with firmness. "We can't expose our children to swearing."

"Will our teenagers work alongside Catholics?" one person asked me. "Of course," I replied. "We can't participate then," she said with firmness.

The woman from this congregation was exhibiting purity in a culture she judged to be immoral. Such sectarianism is a key feature of fundamentalism. Her lack of respect that in a heavily Catholic neighborhood a visitor at her church might be a serious Catholic with two Catholic teenage children is typical of the fundamentalist mindset.

In our respective approaches to the Bible, I am likewise 180 degrees removed from fundamentalism.

Each semester, for example, I try to moderate a Christian student club at the community college where I teach. Last semester's experience reflects what happens virtually every year. About eight students came to my office after seeing my flyer announcing the formation of the club. I opened with a short prayer, using a passage from The Acts of the Apostles. I explained the three purposes of the club: to provide mutual support and some socializing, to have some faith formation, and to sponsor a modest service project on campus. I emphasized that this is a student-led club that needs a simple charter signed by twelve students for entry into the interclub council.

One of the students, Lance, spoke next. "We should introduce ourselves," he began. "I'll start with a prayer and then tell why I'm here." Apparently the opening prayer I offered wasn't good enough for Lance. His prayer and witness took nearly ten minutes. Lance's friend then gave us an involved, heartfelt witness. The other students—all Catholics—gave their names and said something about their class schedules. Lance then quickly raised a point about club membership. "We should welcome all students who have been saved," he said.

"Do we include Catholics?" I asked.

"Not," said Lance, "unless they want to be saved." Lance then distributed some tracts on the "correct" interpretation of some Bible passages that emphasized, "The Bible is true, word for word."

The club, as far as I was concerned, could not proceed with Lance in it. Actually, Lance never really wanted to charter a student club, which at a public college means open membership. The Catholic students were turned off by the whole thing, but they were not savvy enough to realize what was happening or how to deal with it. Over the next few weeks I buttonholed several of the Catholic students, challenging them to try again for an inclusive group. (For the record, another teacher moderates a respectful evangelical student group on campus. Lance, I learned, tried to subvert it in the same way.)

The Bible and Me

Lance is hardly the rare person. ABC News Prime Time recently surveyed people in this country on their attitude about the Bible. Just over 60 percent consider biblical accounts, even including the Noah's ark story and the six-day creation story, "to be true, word for word." It surprised me, however, that nearly 50 percent of Catholics agreed.

My own experience as a college student years ago stands in stark contrast to that of Lance and to the ABC survey. A few days after my freshmen registration, I found myself in a course called "New Testament" that transformed my life and enabled my vocation.

The teacher happened to be a diocesan priest, although lay people taught other sections of the course. The priest was not particularly *liberal*. He received some graduate education in Europe and was being groomed for some promotion. So my reaction to the course wasn't because the teacher was *far out* or, if I accurately recall, even because he was particularly insightful.

I simply had never before—and this will sound stupid—realized that the New Testament had a plot. I didn't know that the life and arrest and death of Jesus had a political, religious, cultural and historical context. Yes, from about fifth grade I had a sense that the liturgical cycle went from December birth to spring resurrection. Yes, in seventh grade I drew a map of St. Paul's journeys using colored pencils. Yes, I had my own Bible in high school, and it probably came with a chronology. Yes, some of the preaching in my parish was Scripture-based, to a degree. Until that college course, however, I had always presumed that the Bible was a collection of isolated incidents that may or may not apply to the isolated incidents of my life.

I had never before seen that each of the four gospels stressed different themes. I had never before seen a climax in the story, a turning point (at Caesarea Philippi, for example), after which the story moves inevitably to a conclusion. I never heard that the Romans oppressed the Jews who, in turn, were was divided on how to react to the occupation. To tell the truth, I had never before heard that Jesus was a Jew. No one concealed that fact from me, but no one ever mentioned it.

I had never before considered that some passages in the Bible seemingly contradict others. I had never heard of independent Jewish or Roman writers who commented upon Jesus or the early Christians. I did not know there were other noncanonical writings, somewhat similar to those in the New Testament. I didn't even realize there were different Bible translations, sometimes using different sources. I understood for the first time that a Bible passage mentioning Jesus' "brothers," for example, might raise questions among some Christians about the perpetual virginity of Mary and that several Catholic doctrines (such as the Immaculate Conception and the Assumption) are not derived directly from the Bible.

I'm embarrassed to admit all this, but I was not unique among my fellow Catholic college students, nor among most adult Catholics of that time.

The upgrade in Catholic appreciation of the Bible was, of course, a belated response to Martin Luther's reform of the Church. Many Catholics in the sixteenth century were obviously attracted to Luther's ideas about the Bible and other matters. But some of those who stayed within the Catholic church also tried to make reforms. In the early 1700s, for example, a small movement inside Catholicism circulated some ideas about the Bible:

- It should be printed in native languages, not just in Latin.
- It should be printed in affordable editions, not just ornamental copies.
- Lay Catholics should devote time to the Bible on Sunday evening.
- People should clearly hear the Scripture proclaimed at Sunday Mass.

In 1713, Pope Clement XI decided to reply to these seemingly innocuous ideas about the Bible. Here is what he said in his statement, *Unigenitus*: "[These ideas about the Bible are] false, captious, ill-sounding, offensive to pious ears, scandalous, pernicious, rash, injurious to the Church and its practices, not only outrageous against the Church but even against secular powers, seditious, impious, blasphemous, suspected of heresy and savoring heresy and lastly also heretical." Clement was simply, though redundantly, reflecting common Catholic attitude of his time: The Bible was the preserve of the institutional Church and was to be read, if at all, in light of official Church teachings.

My college course in the New Testament initially impressed upon me the discrepancies between the Jesus of history and the Christ of faith, between what "really happened" and what the Church was teaching, at least as I understood that teaching. As a college student, I was naturally attuned to the new and unusual rather than to the enormous continuity between what the Church had long taught and what I was learning about the Bible.

This course motivated me to read scores and scores of books on "the quest for the historical Jesus." This line of inquiry was and is for me a confrontation between my simple faith and the tools of science and reason. Although my study in this area leads to doubts, it is necessary and ultimately very growth promoting for me. There are, it seems to me, only three choices for any educated Catholic:

- To relegate the Bible and religion to the realm of fables or vague ethics or unimportance and to accept the secularization thesis, leaving religion at home on Monday morning.
- To become a fundamentalist, presumably enduring intellectual and spiritual schizophrenia at some level.
- To seriously wrestle with the tensions between reason and faith, perhaps reaching intellectual and spiritual harmony after considerable confusion and doubt.

I thank God every day that I have chosen the third option. And I thank the Church for proposing this course of action for me so many years ago.

Getting Help from a Marxist

I received help in my quest for an intelligent Christianity from an unlikely source. Milan Machovec, an atheist, was a Czech philosopher involved for many years in the Christian-Marxist dialogue movement—another topic of interest to me. In his book, *A Marxist Looks At Jesus* (Fortress Press, 1972), Machovec draws attention to Luke 22:32, a passage in which Jesus addresses Peter (and by extension all Christian leaders): "I pray that your faith may not fail; and once you have turned back, you must strengthen and build up the faith of your brethren." The verb *turn back* or *turn again*, writes Machovec, is "the most important clue for understanding Calvary and what happened subsequently!"

It is Peter's faith, Machovec implies, that made a historical tragedy (Calvary) into a victory (the resurrection). As an atheist, Machovec doesn't believe in the resurrection. But his purpose is not to disprove it. He is simply and profoundly pointing out that hundreds or thousands of people saw Jesus in Galilee and Jerusalem, scores saw him die at Calvary. But only those with resurrection faith "came to believe" that Jesus is the Christ, our Lord and our God.

For me, this means that while the quest for the historical Jesus is important, the object of my faith is something different. I believe in what the Church "came to believe." I believe in Jesus as he came to be understood as the Christ. In other words, I believe in Christianity.

After thinking it over, after "turning back," I have come to believe that Christianity correctly understands Jesus as he always was and always will be.

Luke Timothy Johnson, a conservative biblical scholar, states my conclusion in fuller terms in *The Real Jesus* (Harper Collins, 1996). Johnson acknowledges that the historical details of Jesus' life and early Christianity are very important. But "Christian faith has never—either at the start or now—been based on historical reconstructions of Jesus," he writes. Without in any way disputing that Jesus rose from the dead, Johnson emphasizes that the resurrection "is not simply something that happened to Jesus but is equally something that happened to Jesus' followers."

In other words, simply reading the Bible literally cannot reveal the fullness of a dogma such as that of the Trinity.

My study of Christian history further convinces me that the Catholic developmental approach to dogma is sound, even when dogmatic formulations go beyond the biblical events of ancient Judaism and early Christianity. For example, passages on the divinity of Jesus and on the Trinity can be found in the Bible. But as the Arian controversy in the early church made evident, there are enough Bible passages to plausibly argue against the current formulations of these dogmas.

Our foundational Christian dogmas, as Richard Rubenstein details in *When Jesus Became God* (Harcourt, 1999), are the result of a fair amount of philosophical debate and even political maneuvering. In other words, simply reading the Bible literally cannot reveal the fullness of a dogma such as that of the Trinity. Yes, some fundamentalists might find the Trinity in their reading of the Bible. But on that topic and many others, fundamentalists read Bible passages quite selectively. It is no coincidence that some fundamentalists are quite fuzzy on the Trinity and even—when I listen to them closely—on Jesus' divinity (to highlight only these two foundational beliefs of our faith).

By the way, during my study of the Arian heresy, I was impressed to learn that the laity, not always the hierarchy, carried the correct teaching on Jesus' divinity through Christianity's early years. Rubenstein quotes from a talk by Gregory of Nyssa from 381 A.D.: "If in this city you ask a shopkeeper for change, he will argue with you about whether the Son is begotten or unbegotten. If you inquire about the quality of bread, the baker will answer, 'The Father is greater; the Son is less.' And if you ask the bath attendant to draw your bath, he will tell you that the Son was created ex nihilo [out of nothing]." This fascinating ancient quotation, comments Rubenstein, "suggests that ordinary trades people and workers felt perfectly competent—perhaps even driven—to debate abstract theological issues."

Later I learned that in his study of the early Church, Cardinal John Henry Newman—as good a Church leader if there ever was one, even though he has never been canonized—also observed that "the wisdom of the lay faithful" was the definitive carrier of Christianity's correct teaching. How's that for radical ecclesiology?

god quote

Reason and Faith

In his own journey, Lance, the fundamentalist college student, is self-assured—at least for the moment, at least on the outside. My journey is more complex. It probably sounds too academic, overly intellectual. It certainly involves courses and books. But my vocation also includes a healthy personal relationship with Jesus. My response to God, my relationship to Jesus, however, would not be possible without an intellectual approach to my faith. My struggle over approaches to the Bible is an example of how my God-given faith comports with my worldly endeavors, indeed how my faith is enriched by my experiences at the school where I teach, at the parish where I assist, around my home as a husband and father, and in my neighborhood. I am, nearly thirty-five years since my college course on the New Testament, sure that my faith, which admittedly stretches the bounds of history and science at points, is not an unreasonable assent to a body of belief but rather a rational response to a real call.

The 1960 election of President John Kennedy provided my generation with a model of a Catholic layman who was comfortable in modern society. (In my opinion, one reason John Kerry lost the presidential election in 2004 was that he was unable to explain how his faith impacted his vocation as a politician.)

Looking back, Kennedy's famous campaign talk to the Protestant ministers in Houston was more defensive about Catholicism in the public arena than we understood at the time. Still, Kennedy represented a confident Catholicism that was a full partner in our country's democratic experiment. Kennedy was well educated, well read, and very articulate. He surrounded himself with "the best and the brightest" advisors, including Protestants, Jews, and other Catholics, notably his brother Robert. John and Robert Kennedy made it "cool," at least for me, to become an educated Catholic.

The Kennedy presidency and the Camelot mystique that flourished after his death made tangible for me what I had been feeling about a worldly vocation. Unfortunately, the outward-looking confidence of the Kennedy era is losing ground in some corners to a creeping Catholic neo-fundamentalism. This trend threatens my calling in and to the world.

The term *Catholic neo-fundamentalism* implies continuity with the Protestant fundamentalism that appeared in 1920, but it is also different. Both types of Christian fundamentalism, in turn, have similarities and differences with fundamentalism within Islam, as will be discussed later.

This is not the first time Catholics have swayed between a confident outlook toward the world and a retrenchment. In the thirteenth century, for example, new thinkers like St. Thomas Aquinas and others tried to integrate faith with reason, but they were opposed by some Catholics who preferred mindless practices and even authoritarianism.

Today, to pick one issue, some Catholic leaders are worried that the Vatican II openness to other faith traditions leaves the impression that no one religion is closer to the truth than another. In fact, some of those people say Vatican II has backfired: that in the post-Vatican II era too many people construct faith *cafeteria style*—a little from here and a little from there.

My experience does not support the conclusion of these worriers, though I very much share their concern. Yes, many of my college students who were baptized Catholic know shockingly little about their religion. Yes, some young adults embrace a New Age approach to spirituality, mixing bits and pieces. But the fault does not lie with Vatican II or with ecumenical dialogue, and the remedy is certainly not an updated version of triumphal Catholicism. To the contrary, the likelihood of my students discovering a truly Catholic vocation for themselves is proportionate to the distance they keep from any expression of fundamentalism.

1 800 377 0095

Tri Vita
Sublingual B-12 System

Catholic Neo-Fundamentalists

Although it is a significant movement within our Church in this country and more so overseas, I directly encounter Catholic neo-fundamentalism only sporadically.

For example, some months ago, at the invitation of a fellow teacher, I attended a presentation about globalization at a nearby parish. A young adult couple had just returned from a demonstration at an international summit in Seattle. Their key word was *resistance*. My colleague, whose daughter volunteers in a clinic in Panama, asked the young couple for an economic analysis as a basis for their protest. "Read the Bible," the husband asserted. He was not about to be touched by questions of strategy or consideration of trade-offs.

The supposition that the Bible yields specific direction on globalization without the filters of reason, science, history and human experience is a characteristic of neo-fundamentalism. The young couple speaking about resistance in Seattle is on the left. The same neo-fundamentalist misuse of the Bible is employed on the right.

For example, a diocesan official once told me that women are excluded from the ordained priesthood in Roman Catholicism because "there's nothing in the Bible to indicate that Jesus ordained women." Such a silly argument, I countered, jeopardizes many Catholic positions not found directly in the Bible, including opposition to slavery, support of labor unions, and infant baptism. Catholics are not fundamentalists, I reminded the chancery official. If there is a truly Catholic reason for a male-only priesthood, it isn't because the guests at the Last Supper were male—even in the unlikely event that they were!

Catholic neo-fundamentalists are falling into the simplistic trap of *What Would Jesus Do?* Taken literally, the slogan is practically worthless. The Bible, unaided by tradition and reason, does not give exact answers on foreign policy, the delivery of human services, or even on family dilemmas. Therein lies the humor and wisdom of G.K. Chesterton's reply when asked to name the book he would most enjoy were he stranded on a deserted island. He bypassed the Bible in favor of *The Idiot's Guide to Practical Shipbuilding.*

There is a faction in a downstate Illinois church that constantly denigrates every homily and every parish program. They badger the pastor, a friend of mine, for more devotional services. Only more devotional services, they say, will bring people into the true faith.

Last year the pastor of this church recruited a handful of high school students to conduct the Stations of the Cross on Fridays during Lent. This should have pleased the neo-fundamentalist faction on two counts: The Stations are a traditional devotion and young people are involved. But the faction became more upset than ever because the teens made the Stations "too modern." For example, when Jesus falls under the weight of the cross, the teens prayed for an end to discrimination against gays in their school.

This incident exposes more features of creeping Catholic neo-fundamentalism. It is always against something but never capable of organizing a vibrant alternative. It harkens back to a golden age (in this case, the time before Vatican II was supposedly perfect) and tries to restore that golden age by focusing on small matters (more devotions, for example), while doing nothing about the substantial (such as the religious illiteracy of today's Catholic young people).

A final humorous instance of my travails with neo-fundamentalism involves an exchange with a center in Canada that supposedly fosters devotion to Our Blessed Lady. It sent me an urgent e-mail expressing "outrage" over a "scandalous project" to open the Fatima Shrine in Portugal to "Muslims…and other pagans." The center wants me to lobby for a *Catholics-only* policy at the Portugal shrine.

Among its several errors, the center seemed unaware that the shrine in Portugal is named after a daughter of the prophet Muhammad: Fatima. I likewise informed them that Mary, the virgin mother of Jesus, is highly revered by Muslims. She is mentioned in many passages in the Qur'an. I also told them that Portugal had been, for a time, a Muslim country. A Muslim leader in Portugal had a daughter named Fatima after whom he named the town. She married a Catholic, leading to some harmony in Portugal between Muslims and Catholics.

Why in 1917 did Our Lady appear in an insignificant village in Portugal? In an old book, *The World's First Love* (Image Books, 1952), Bishop Fulton Sheen (formerly my bishop in Rochester) says, "The Blessed Virgin chose to be known as *Our Lady of Fatima* precisely as a pledge and a sign of hope to the Muslim people."

This incident illustrates the Catholic neo-fundamentalist hostility to other faith traditions. It also, in my opinion, betrays the anti-intellectualism in the movement.

It is, admittedly, anxiety provoking to reach beyond one's little circle. Any serious encounter between two or more religions, cultures or families is a crisis of some sort. But the outcome, as I have experienced in my extended family (which through marriage includes Protestants and Jews) and through my work, can be a strengthening of faith, of culture, of family life.

The process is not magic. Simply, for example, putting Christians and Muslims in a seminar room does not automatically cause mutual respect and a deepening of faith, no more than simply putting blacks and whites in the same school magically advances racial harmony. Competent dialogue leaders are a necessary part of the vision. So too are experienced teachers and savvy community organizers. But under the right conditions, my vocation tells me, people who engage in respectful dialogue (either in a formal interreligious group or by cooperating with others on civic issues) will deepen their own faith and effectively share the truth.

My Vocation after September 11, 2001

The murderous attack on our country was a tragedy for families, friends and fellow citizens of the innocent victims. It was a tragedy for all civilized people. Because the murders were committed in the name of religion, September 11th was also a setback for all of us who believe that religion should be a force for good in society. "The events of that day," says Wilfred McClay of the University of Tennessee, confirm for some people the "contention that religion is incorrigibly toxic, and that it breeds irrationality, demonization of others, irreconcilable division, and implacable conflict." The attack bolsters the argument that religion "should be kept private and tethered to a short leash."

Does Islam really condone the murder of innocent passengers, workers, civil servants, and pedestrians? Emphatically not! Thousands of Muslims in this country and millions in nearly every other country have repeatedly condemned the murderous terrorism of September 11, 2001. There is no need, in my opinion, to proof-text the Qur'an for abhorrence to despicable murder. All moral people are unequivocally opposed to cowardly attacks of terrorism as a means of achieving an end (although I will concede that we Catholics have committed our fair share of terrorism over the years, but never when we were true to our faith).

That being said, it is permissible to ask: Does Islam hate North American culture? Is there legitimacy in hundreds of newspaper headlines like "Islam vs. the Modern West"? The complex and multifarious answer holds the future of Islam and perhaps the future of our world.

Please understand that my strong belief in the beneficent engagement between people of faith and modern society does not mean that Christianity or Islam should embrace modernity uncritically. Religious traditions are wise to recognize conflict between a wholesome, holy life and runaway Western values. Indeed, some strains in religion are now morally bankrupt because of an over-accommodation with modernity. Some expressions of Christianity, Islam and Judaism have allowed people to feel morally secure with individualism, capitalism, consumerism and ethical relativism.

> *It would be self-defeating and a betrayal of my God-given call to live in fear and resentment, to be imprisoned by a language of resistance.*

Nonetheless, a starting point for my vocation is love for my society. It would be self-defeating and a betrayal of my God-given call to live in fear and resentment, to be imprisoned by a language of resistance. In a sense, my vocation comes down to making a way between total accommodation to modernity, called *secularism*, and reactionary fundamentalism. Both extremes are unhealthy for modern culture, for religion, and for me.

Because I have long taught a college course in World Religion, I am involved with the Muslim students on campus. For the same reasons, I am often asked to speak about Islam to Christian groups or in interreligious settings. I always make the point that the responsibility of bringing Islam to bear on the issues of the day falls primarily to Muslims. Their sophisticated task, I explain, is delicate because they hold that the Qur'an was revealed word-for-word, because Muslim dogma sometimes has an ahistorical flavor, and for other reasons. There are, however, philosophers, teachers, students and workers in Indonesia, Iran, Morocco, France, the United States and elsewhere who are part of a critical engagement between Islam and modernity. This process is occurring in my neighborhood and at my college. Formally and informally, I have been privileged to eavesdrop.

When people mention a *golden age of Islam*, what they might have in mind is Baghdad in the late eighth through ninth centuries. Back then, Baghdad could boast of over 100 paper manufacturers, while Europeans were writing on stone or parchment, if at all. In fact, paper was so abundant in Arabia it was usually free, allowing ordinary people access to literature and the news. Long ago, Baghdad developed mathematics (particularly algebra), advancements in medicine (including sophisticated hospitals), philosophy, and much more.

Arabia achieved these things, explains Peter Watson in *The Modern Mind* (Harper Collins, 2002), by reaching out to the wider world, by adapting and building upon the ideas of others. Arabia borrowed technology for paper from China; ideas about hospitals from Persia; math from India; philosophy from Greece. The so-called *golden age* of Islam, contrary to the defensiveness of today's fundamentalists, was a product of openness to others. "More prosperity comes from openness, receptivity and curiosity than from the closed, self-referential world of fundamentalist religions," Watson concludes.

On November 18, 2001, I chaperoned a busload of teenagers from Maria High School to the refurbished Navy Pier on Chicago's lakefront. There 2,000 Christians and people of other faiths joined 2,000 Muslims for the largest interreligious dialogue ever held in our city.

My friend, Greg Pierce, with others from a group called United Power for Action and Justice paired us off for one-to-one conversations at Navy Pier. The event was tense at first—at least I felt tense after riding a bus with forty high school students—but the conversations were enlightening as we met fellow Chicagoans who share our concerns and hopes. The event at Navy Pier, just weeks after the murderous attack on our country, was a solid rebuke to Osama bin Laden and others who desire nothing but to breed fear and to turn people against one another.

I love this country. We argue constantly about our differences. Although some of our disagreements are based on fear and phobias, we (*e pluribus unum*) are quite capable of treating fellow citizens and fellow members of the human family with dignity. The months around the September 11, 2001, tragedy saw an outpouring of the best in my fellow citizens. During those days, contrary to the hope of bin Laden, the percentage of people in this country holding "a favorable view of Islam" actually *increased* by 15 percent to just shy of 60 percent. That increase, as much as any military response to al Qaeda, is the redemption of Ground Zero. That increase, as reported by the Pew Research Center, is a direct consequence of efforts such as that at Navy Pier. Subsequently, I have participated in similar Christian and Muslim dialogues at my college, Moraine Valley, and at another nearby college, Trinity Christian. My own parish, Sacred Heart, has likewise sponsored a few interreligious events, including a Seder Supper with Jews, Christians and Muslims.

My personal vocation is discerned by sharp auditory reception to current events. My spiritual antennae are turned in the direction of breaking news reports. This does not mean that I make up my faith anew in each situation. But I am guided by advice attributed to Karl Barth: Leave the house in the morning with a Bible in one pocket and the newspaper in another. Central to my vocation is reciprocity between ordinary people and history in the making. Late twentieth and early twenty-first century events have made me who I am as a Christian. Simultaneously, like-minded friends and I have made late twentieth and early twenty-first century history, and our children will continue the job we have begun.

Taking a Winding Road to Chicago

Interstate 90 directly connects Rochester to Chicago, not counting an interstate spur through the Rochester suburbs. My move to Chicago in 1978 was thus a straight drive, but the journey was circuitous.

Following the 1964 race riot in Rochester, I gradually got involved in the issues of the day, particularly the peace movement. My calling was saying to me: "Christianity belongs in the public square. Christians can improve society!"

My participation in peace demonstrations was a natural response to my vocation. At that time, Father Daniel Berrigan, SJ, was stationed at Cornell University, a morning's drive from my own college. With his brother Phillip, a Josephite priest, and a handful of others, Berrigan courageously, creatively and prophetically protested the Vietnam War through civil disobedience. Particularly because they were Catholic priests, the Berrigans greatly appealed to me.

The Berrigans chose to go around the system and above normal channels in their opposition to the war. The Berrigans were not interested in electoral candidates or in Congressional legislation. They preached "pure resistance" through prophetic action.

Like other movements, the peace movement was heavy on moralizing, which at first fit perfectly with my sense of vocation. But after a while, I found myself thinking a lot about effectiveness, about strategy and tactics. Don't get me wrong. The peace movement wasn't an either/or choice between a moral stance and a compromising political campaign. My participation in the movements certainly included political events, advocacy for legislation, and more. However, the movements, at least within my exposure, lacked the institutional means to articulate long-term programs.

That's how Catholics are: Even if we don't agree with you, we prize relationships over ideology and want you to follow your dreams to the end.

My reflection returned to our town's 1964 race riot and the churches' subsequent decision to hire Saul Alinsky's Industrial Areas Foundation (IAF). I read Alinsky's books, looking for guidance about my vocation in advocating social change. I also searched for an intellectual connection between social action and the Catholic tradition.

In 1970, I headed to Chicago for three months at the IAF training center on Michigan Avenue, run by Alinsky's heir apparent, Ed Chambers. Chambers had been the lead organizer for FIGHT in Rochester. I had met him when I was a teenager, but I'm sure he didn't remember me. My pastor in Irondequoit, although opposed to involving churches in power politics, gave me $300 for the tuition. (That's how Catholics are: Even if we don't agree with you, we prize relationships over ideology and want you to follow your dreams to the end.)

The IAF preached the importance of effectiveness when working for social justice, drawing a sharp distinction between its approach and the "say all the right things but don't get your own hands dirty in the real world" attitude found in some movements. During that summer I learned that the organizing method of the IAF was partially derived from the *observe-judge-act* inquiry method of Catholic Action, developed in 1913 by Cardinal Joseph Cardijn in Belgium. Monsignor Reynold

Hillenbrand and Monsignor Jack Egan of Chicago, among others, later brought this social inquiry method to the United States.

For the fall semester I was back in Rochester, eager to read the actual documents of Vatican II and rummage through other collections of Catholic social teaching and commentaries on Catholic morality. Frequently, the example used to illustrate one or another point was taken from Chicago. For the next few years I was regularly in and out of Chicago, keeping some contact with the IAF.

I realized what was happening: My vocation was telling me that Christians not only need to be involved in the world but also have to become *effective* agents for change. I was being called to connect substantially with Catholic social thinking, particularly its Chicago embodiment. With a goal, but no job, at age twenty-something I drove my car onto the westbound lane of Interstate 90, hoping to hook up somehow with the no-nonsense, results-oriented, social-change spirit of the Windy City.

Discouragement awaited me. Without checking with me, the IAF had recently moved its national headquarters to Long Island. It was ironic that I left the state of New York to seek something that had just moved to the state of New York. I was not tempted to turn around, however.

I eventually met Professor Russ Barta at Mundelein College, now part of Loyola University in Chicago. He was involved, among many things, with Catholic labor schools. He was an expert on all aspects of Vatican II, having designed update courses for hundreds of priests, religious and laity in the late 1960s.

Through Barta I met many of the other people associated with Catholic social action in Chicago, starting with his wife Bernice Barta, her brother Ed Marciniak and his wife Virginia, Monsignors Dan Cantwell, George Higgins and Jack Egan, Patty Crowley, John and Theresa McDermott, Larry Ragan, Father Dennis Geaney, OSA, Vaile and Mary Scott, Peggy Roach, Peter Foote, Marty Burns, Tom and Kay

Gaudette, Anne Zimmerman, and many more. From these people I heard stories about the Catholic Labor Alliance, the Christian Family Movement, the Young Christian Workers, the Young Christian Students, the monthly *Work* newspaper, the Catholic Interracial Council, the Cana Conference, St. Benet's Bookshop, the Adult Education Centers, Chicago Inter-Student Catholic Action (CISCA), the Office of Urban Affairs, the Catholic Committee on Urban Ministry, and other Catholic social justice efforts that had graced the Chicago archdiocese.

The themes of my street-level education in social action, Chicago-style, are now so engrained that it is hard for me to explain the *before-and-after*. Nor should I imply that the Midwest phase of my vocation is in discontinuity with my calling from fifth grade through college. Moving to Chicago, however, was a clear decision on my part to downplay my moral certainty in favor of contemplating the more ambiguous role of ordinary people in improving the mediating institutions of their lives.

Chicago-style social action champions "insiders" and is wary of "outsiders." This has nothing to do with where you come from, but it has everything to do with where you find the locus of your vocation. According to my Chicago mentors, Christians must simultaneously be both insiders and outsiders in society. The outsider thoroughly goads the system through protest, sometimes including civil disobedience. The outsider's denunciation of society's flaws is absolutely needed. But Chicago was unique in highlighting the role of insiders—people who work quietly inside the organizations of government, business and Church to help make them more like the kingdom of God. Insiders, I learned, can be every bit as allergic to injustice as the most rabble-rousing prophet you can imagine.

The insider, always on alert for strategic openings, attends to the rules and standards that govern various facets of life. The insider is obsessed with the creation, operation and ongoing reform of institutions.

The insider's approach to social change fascinates me because, frankly, the surety and moralizing in the outsider's approach was turning me off. That revulsion was never stronger than when I encountered my own shadow.

Many Christian activists, including many Church employees, station themselves outside or against the system. They know how to condemn war, exploitation, pollution, racism, consumerism, abortion and other sins rightly condemned. But they haven't a clue how to challenge and encourage business managers, labor leaders, government officials, social service and health care administrators, educators at every level, and others who incrementally construct peace and justice all week long.

A Remarkable Document

I n 1977, just a year before my arrival, several veterans of Chicago-style social action had issued *A Chicago Declaration of Christian Concern*. They were upset that too much of the Church's language and practice was being focused on the outsiders in the church and not enough attention was being paid to the insiders—which included most of the laity. Here is what the *Chicago Declaration* said:

> We note the steady depreciation within the last decade of the ordinary social roles through which the laity serve and act upon the world. The impression is often created that one can work for justice and peace only by stepping outside of these ordinary roles as a business person, as a mayor, as a factory worker, as a professional in the State Department, or as an active union member and thus that one can change the system only as an outsider to the society and the system.
>
> Such ideas clearly depart from the mainstream of Catholic social thought, which regards the advance of social justice as essentially the service performed within one's professional and occupational milieu. The almost exclusive preoccupation with the role of the *outsider* as the model of social action can only distract the laity from the

apostolic potential that lies at the core of their professional and occupational lives.

In 1978, the signers of this *Declaration* started the National Center for the Laity (NCL). I joined the NCL board in about 1980 at the invitation of its first president, Russ Barta, by then my teacher in graduate school and my mentor. I have been involved in NCL ever since. I edit its newsletter, *INITIATIVES*, which chronicles ways ordinary Christians link their faith to their work—on the job, around the home, and in the neighborhood. I've also written two books on faith and work and five booklets, each about the spirituality of a specific occupation.

Notice, in the section quoted above, the *Declaration's* use of the term *social justice*. It is a phrase that is commonly used in church circles and elsewhere. Yet a reexamination of the virtue itself, I regularly argue, might go a long way to advancing the actual practice of social justice.

The unique activity of social justice is organizing like-minded people to improve policies or institutions. Picket lines and other means of protest can set the stage for social justice, but the two are not to be equated. In fact, although the virtue of social justice is nearly always controversial, it usually happens without any protest at all.

Pursuing the Chicago definition of *social justice* has put me in conflict with many Church employees and others who define working for justice as primarily an outside activity. For example, I recently chided a Church employee for writing that as the director of the diocesan Office for Peace and Justice he is "in charge of peace and justice issues." I contend that peace and justice will best be advanced if laypeople of all walks of life take the initiative for justice among like-minded workers, not waiting one second for cues from the director of the Office for Peace and Justice—or anyone else, for that matter.

Don't get me wrong. Church employees have a role to play in teaching the virtues of peace and justice. But what should they be doing?

For starters they should quit speaking as if they represent all Christians in a city, state or Church jurisdiction. Too many Church employ-ees are in the habit of saying—to the press, to legislators, to fellow parishioners—that they represent *the* Catholic position. For example, a Church employee recently lobbied the Illinois legislature on hog farm-ing, quoting an encyclical while claiming to speak "for all the dioceses in Illinois." Except on a very clear-cut moral matter (certainly not hog farming), it is quite possible that sincere and informed Christian citizens have a different position from the Church employee.

> Church employees can similarly teach peace and justice by not using nouns like diocese or church interchangeably with themselves.

Church employees can similarly teach peace and justice by not using nouns like *dio-cese* or *church* interchangeably with themselves. It is one thing for the director of a chancery peace and justice office to write a letter to the editor on public housing. It is something else, however, when the letter with its specific policy ideas claims to be "the position of the Church, which knows the future of public housing."

The *sine qua non* of my model of Christian living, which I believe is exactly what Vatican II proposed, is a new understanding of the church-in-the-world and a refurbished notion of the laity. Obviously, the model of a lay-centered church is broad and generic. Concrete cir-cumstances vary in different societies, even in different neighbor-hoods. But the refreshing vision of Vatican II dims each time we laypeople have to look over our shoulders to the rectory or the chancery for cues on matters in which we are eminently competent. Twenty-first-century Christians construct peace and justice by attend-ing to the hundreds of daily decisions that confront us.

Church employees who sincerely want to promote peace and justice (and there are many) can sponsor forums in which workers, parents and neighbors reflect on their experience and make judgments on their institutions. Church employees can also agitate ordinary Christians who are tempted by apathy to say, "You can't fight city hall" or "You can't change hospital rules." The Church employees might facilitate gatherings of like-minded workers and neighbors who desire change without, however, telling them what to do.

Pioneering a Spirituality
of Work

My friend and colleague, Greg Pierce, describes himself as "piety impaired." He's a busy north side Chicago publisher and businessman, husband, father, community activist, and Cubs fan who wants "a spirituality of noise, crowds and complexity." Instead he hears sermons about "getting away from the world to discover God" and about the spiritual superiority of "silence, solitude and simplicity."

Christian spirituality, Pierce contends, has been packaged in language and images that direct people away from their work. He points out that the term *holy place*, for example, is assumed to be "where some other-worldly experience happens—usually in church or on a mountaintop or in a desert. And yet we may just as likely feel the presence of God in our office or over the kitchen table or at a political rally, but we would normally not dub those *holy places*."

Is there a spiritual language and a set of disciplines suited for people who work for a living, who raise children, who attend to their marriage?

In the early 1980s, I was organizing unemployed workers in my neighborhood. I was told to meet an expert at such activity, Father Dennis Geaney, OSA. From that moment until he died in November

1992, Geaney was a frequent visitor to our home. After suffering a heart attack, Geaney developed the habit of taking long walks in the town of Calumet City and elsewhere. Along the way he would stop in small factories, auto repair shops, agencies, and homes. What he gleaned from those walks helped Geaney articulate a spirituality for the laity in his sermons, in his books, and in a weekly bulletin column he titled "Confessions of a Streetwalker."

There are "disastrous consequences," Geaney warns, if lay spirituality is simply something borrowed from the monastery.

A genuine spirituality for the laity, says Geaney, would "seem at first to be the opposite of what the classical spiritual writers call *the conversion to God* because lay spirituality in our times requires a *conversion to the world*. Too many people like to shy away from the world when they become reconverted to God. Too often they want to love God away from the stock exchange, courts of justice, factories, offices, or marts of trade."

Many of the dominant themes in Christian spirituality derive from a monastic tradition, Geaney said. To be fair, work has a place in that tradition. But for monks, work is a backdrop to contemplation, a tool for prayer. This leads to a spirituality in which good intentions are often more important than competent action.

There are "disastrous consequences," Geaney warns, if lay spirituality is simply something borrowed from the monastery. For the laity, work *in and of itself* must count. Work is not to be merely tolerated; it is a call "to complete the work of creation and to cooperate in the work of redemption.... Work itself must become a way to God, not merely an interlude between morning and evening prayers. In fact, prayer cannot be defined as time snatched from the messy world.... Every bed made, potato peeled, or ton of steel poured is the incense of praise to God rising above the suburban chimney and the black clouds of the steel mill." An incense-filled chapel is no more holy than a smoke-filled caucus room. A sin-scarred world is, for a full-time Christian like me, as much a place for holiness as any monastery.

Kathleen Norris, a popular poet and spiritual writer, was once invited to be a guest homilist. The pastor told her "to focus on personal spirituality." But as Norris prepared the sermon she realized "that the whole notion of a personal spirituality [is] an impossibility, a contradiction in terms." When the word *personal* is used in a religious context, the meaning is usually *private*. "But Christianity, like its ancestor Judaism, is inescapably communal," says Norris. "I've...become increasingly wary of what strikes me as a growing tendency to treat the soul as just one more [individual] consumer on the American landscape and spirituality as the commodity that fulfills every whim."

This focus on personal spirituality comes to North America by way of Protestantism, especially its Calvinist influences. To say that Christians on this continent restrict spirituality to an inward journey does not mean they are selfish. In fact, North American Christians are exemplary in their willingness to build and support church-sponsored schools, hospitals and agencies. North American Christians, as individuals and as congregations, send donations to every corner of the globe. Yet, when it comes to prayer and the spiritual life, I've observed that North American Christians consider their faith to be "a private matter between God and me."

Pop psychology and the New Age movement support this individualistic pietism by implying that wisdom is nothing more than the fulfillment of personal potential with little attention to broader social concerns. Many North Americans, as they move away from immigrant enclaves, adopt a totally individualistic approach to spirituality, what has been called "Starbuck's Christianity."

In Chicago, however, I found a tradition of another kind of spirituality—one in which we, in the company of others, encounter God in the give and take of marriage, family life, business, civic endeavors, and worldly affairs. The United States Catholic bishops refer to this type of spirituality in their pastoral letter, *Economic Justice For All*:

> Holiness is not limited to the sanctuary or to moments of private prayer; it is a call to direct our whole heart and life toward God and according to God's plan for the world. For the laity holiness is achieved in the midst of the world, in family, in community, in friendships, in work, in leisure, in citizenship...
>
> We need a spirituality that calls forth and supports lay initiative and witness not just in our churches but also in business, in the labor movement, in the professions, in education and in public life. Our faith is not just a weekend obligation, a mystery to be celebrated around the altar on Sunday. It is a pervasive reality to be practiced everyday in homes, offices, factories, schools and businesses across our land.

This type of spirituality, designed for busy Christians on the job, in the family, and around the neighborhood, is being called *the spirituality of work*. My Chicago friends have not hammered out all its details, nor have they tried to corner the market. They are simply and profoundly experimenting with a way of being holy from Monday through Saturday.

A Chicago Catholic, I've learned, knows the importance of saying prayers, especially through the liturgy. But just saying prayers is not the same thing as being a prayerful person. In fact, in Chicago we don't usually *say* prayers all day long. Instead we make a Morning Offering—giving all our "works, joys and sufferings of this day" to God—so that we can go about our business competently without further spiritualizing our activities. This spirituality of work, in our opinion, is as legitimate a spiritual path as any other.

Some Spiritual Rules

Here in a sketchy, random and incomplete list are seven rules of Chicago-style spirituality of work, as gleaned from my experience:

Rule 1: Take work and public life very seriously. At the same time, don't take life's inevitable conflicts too personally. (I'm discussing public life here, but I've also learned that the art of raising teenagers is not to take family life too personally either.)

One winter morning on my way to teaching at Loyola University, I stopped in Ed Marciniak's office only to catch the tail end of an angry phone argument he was having with Monsignor Jack Egan over some matter. I was startled to hear very sharp barbs on one end, presumably equally matched at Egan's end. I was sure their long friendship was over. After class I stopped by Egan's office with an unexpressed desire to reconcile my two heroes.

"Want to go to lunch?" I asked Egan.

"Sure," he replied. "But hold on a minute. A sensitive public housing issue has come up. I've got to make a couple of calls."

Egan first dialed an alderman, if I recall. Then he dialed Marciniak. "Eddy, I'm in a jam," Egan began. "I need your help."

That was it. Fight your opponent hard in the morning; go back as a friend on another issue in the afternoon. This lesson has been very beneficial to my spiritual life. My feelings get hurt just like anyone else. I ruminate over criticisms leveled at me. But I've learned not to rupture relationships over every slight, every disagreement. It's better to be a player who loses some rounds than to score righteous points, only to subsequently be ignored. To live a spirituality of work, it is essential to stay in the game.

> Rule 2: When in doubt, get on a picket line. In other words, soul searching is fine, but oftentimes self-discovery occurs in a crowd or at an action.

Larry Ragan, a Chicago communications executive and civic leader, was once talking about packing a zoning board hearing. Someone mentioned that not everyone on our side was an ideal Christian. "We can't wait for everyone to get their personal act together," said Ragan. "We get people into action and in the process some of us sometimes become holy."

The same lesson struck me while reading *Reviving Ophelia* by Mary Pipher (Putnam, 1994), a best seller about troubled teenage girls. Pipher mentions that some (although certainly not all) girls who resist any type of intervention become open to the goodness within and around them shortly after volunteering in a homeless shelter.

Some spiritual writers advise: Find your inner light; it will then illuminate those around you. In Chicago we say: Get involved with those around you; that's how you find your inner self.

> Rule 3: Simply accept the fact that everyone does everything for mixed motives or multiple motives. A spirituality of work does not require purity of motives.

One evening I was invited to an advanced screening of an inspiring film about Mother Teresa, produced by Malcolm Muggeridge. Joseph Sullivan, the CEO of a Chicago-based agricultural company, was in our group. During the discussion after the film, Russ Barta agitated the crowd by asserting, "Joe does as much to help the poor as Mother Teresa. He helps get chickens to market at affordable prices." Naturally, an argument ensued because everyone knew Sullivan made big bucks.

> *"Joe does as much to help the poor as Mother Teresa. He helps get chickens to market at affordable prices."*

"I'm not saying Sullivan does *more* than Mother Teresa," Barta calmly but persistently explained. "They both have a vocation. They both care about the poor. And they both have ulterior motives."

By the way, how did many of the people at our gathering know that Sullivan made big bucks? Because they were involved in one or another of the causes he supports with his time and money: a woman's college, a major organization for refugees, an inner-city church, and more.

Rule 4: Don't feel that a spirituality of work, which is a legitimate spirituality, means talking in churchy jargon or wearing religiosity on your sleeve.

Thomas Geoghegan is a Chicago labor lawyer, playwright, and author of the classic book *Which Side Are You On? Trying To Be for Labor When It's Flat on Its Back* (Farrar, Straus, 1991). A religious magazine once assigned me to interview Geoghegan. My editor wasn't happy with my submission because it "wasn't religious enough." So I went back to Geoghegan and then added this quote to the magazine profile: "I have a bit of the Catholic sacramental squint on things," Geoghegan said, but "I don't have to discuss my religion overtly. Sometimes a person can ruin a religious or spiritual experience by shouting *Hey, look at this!* Faith is often a fragile, nonverbal thing. It doesn't bear up well under heavy analysis. Too much melodrama can destroy it. I could sense a moment as a resurrection, for example, but I can't analyze it. The event might lend itself to a religious interpretation, but that's not the only way of seeing it."

Larry Ragan, previously mentioned, was an extremely successful communications executive in Chicago. He believed that poor writing is, at least unconsciously, meant to say, "I don't want you to understand this." Drawing upon George Orwell's famous essay, "Politics and the English Language," Ragan associated specific virtues with writing techniques. For example, the active voice is the virtue of responsibility.

Ragan collected samples of bad writing to use at his seminars. "Do you, at least subconsciously, want to keep people away from your organization," he asked? "Then fill your brochure with tired metaphors and specialized jargon." Then, from his sports coat pocket he pulled out a brochure used in RCIA, the Catholic process for welcoming new members. He then asked his audience of business people—Protestants, Jews, Catholics—to explain or define "mystagogy" or "breaking open the word" or "the scrutinies."

> Rule 5: Stay current on what others are thinking. Share ideas. Intellectual laziness is the second sin against a spirituality of work. (The first sin is incompetence.)

Here's an example of the way this rule worked in the circle I was privileged to join: Monsignor George Higgins, a Chicago priest assigned to Washington, sends a marked article off a wire service or from a journal to Ed Marciniak who, in turn, staples a routing list to the article. Each person, maybe after jotting a comment on the cover note, mails the article to the next person. (I was usually near the bottom of about six readers.) A phone call about the article from someone in the circle might follow. An unusually provocative article or any six-week lull in mail service would require a tavern discussion on a Friday evening.

Higgins wasn't the only one to start the process. Five or six articles could be making the rounds at any given time. Likewise, the circle's membership was elastic. If an article warranted wider comment, a Xerox machine entered the process.

Several of the people in my circle have died. But, as some younger Chicago activists can attest, articles are still shared around town—though e-mail attachments are now more common.

> Rule 6: A spirituality of work invites an appreciation for the arts. Chicago is a city for truckers, stock traders, and lab technicians. Chicago is also a city for poets, musicians, the very best architects, and the truckers, traders and technicians who patronize those arts.

A spirituality of work, as Monsignor Dan Cantwell often said, holds "that a living wage is every person's birthright, but so is music, literature and beauty."

There's an Italian restaurant near Greek Town where Cantwell liked to eat. Over lunch I was remarking on the restored art in the church where he assisted. "All art is religious art," Cantwell asserted.

"What if the artist isn't a practicing Christian?" I asked. "What if the subject matter is entirely secular?"

"As long as the artist is true to the subject and doesn't debase people," Cantwell continued, "that's religious art." Then to get me wound up, Cantwell added: "I don't think there's any such thing as a Christian novel or film."

On that last point he was reacting to self-proclaimed Christian writers and filmmakers who seem to have answers before they have lived the questions. There are plenty of novels and excellent films that deal with Christian themes of redemption and hope, Cantwell said. It is practically irrelevant whether the writer, filmmaker or actors are Christian or not. There are many very good "Christian stories" that feature "totally secular" characters and settings.

> Rule 7: A spirituality of work is a liturgical spirituality, one especially devoted to the Eucharist—at least in my experience. After all, the English word *liturgy* comes from a Greek word meaning *the work of the people.*

My Chicago mentors—particularly Monsignor Dan Cantwell, Monsignor Jack Egan, and Ed Marciniak—were very involved in the liturgical renewal movement years before Vatican II. For example, beginning in the late 1940s, Marciniak and his sister Bernice Barta stood at the communion rail with hands extended, anticipating a practice not found in Catholic churches until the late 1960s.

Why are Chicago social-action leaders interested in the liturgy? Because, like Dorothy Day in New York, Catherine de Hueck Doherty in Canada, and Father Virgil Michel, OSB in Minnesota, they see a connection between the liturgy of the word and the liturgy of the world. They equate the real presence of Christ during Mass with the real presence in the mystical body of Christ at work in the world.

This phrase, *the mystical body of Christ,* is part of daily parlance in Chicago's Catholic social-action circles, although it is gradually disappearing in the wider church. Without an understanding of the doctrine of the mystical body, a Eucharistic minister, as commonly happens, might say to a communicant: *This is the Body of Christ; this is the Blood of Christ.*

The Eucharistic minister is not supposed to draw attention exclusively to the consecrated bread and the consecrated wine, however. The correct phrase, *Body of Christ; Blood of Christ,* is intentionally vague. Yes, Christ is present in the Eucharistic elements, but also really present in the people receiving communion and in all the people of God. How can we believe in the real presence of Christ at Mass if we don't believe in his real presence on the job, with our families, and in the neighborhood?

Whence My Spiritual Journey?

Spirituality today is a buzzword heard on Oprah, throughout the self-help movement, in some business settings, and in many church circles. Spirituality in popular terms is always associated with individually constructed peacefulness, serenity and equanimity. It is assumed that spirituality is something one can choose to have or something one can neglect to pursue.

There is, however, a more anthropological approach to spirituality that contradicts the way most North Americans, both liberals and conservatives, now use the term. In the same way that my vocation was given to me, so too people receive a spirituality. That is, there is a spirituality embedded in every culture. The unique institutional cluster of North American institutions, our ethos, is selectively engaging our aesthetic, emotional, imaginative and rational dimensions to give us a North American spirituality—whether we care to recognize it or not.

Let's go back to Chicago's north side where my friend Greg Pierce operates a small business out of a warehouse within walking distance of Wrigley Field. He wants spirituality to make sense within the context of his business, his family life, and his civic involvements. What's so odd about Pierce's request? If *spirituality* primarily means *a way of life*, then there already is a spirituality embedded in the culture of Chicago, and that spirituality is probably noisy, pluralistic, active and very communal. Pierce's quest then is not to construct a spirituality on top of his already hectic life but to pay attention more profoundly to what beckons from the cluster of institutions that surround him. In other words, we cannot invent our own spirituality any more than we can invent our own religion.

The term *spirituality* is, I realize, routinely contrasted with *religion* in this country—precisely to contend that individuals can construct a spiritual life without being bound by religion. That contrast points to a confusion, or better yet a paradox, in our culture.

Liberty is such a foundational theme in North American culture that some type of individuality must, I suspect, be an ingredient in North American spirituality. Any religion on these shores that makes wholesale condemnation of individuality is consigned to irrelevance or bound to be rejected.

Many of my college students say: "I've given up on religion, but I'm still spiritual." Some of them are rationalizing their lack of curiosity and discipline. But those who are sincere often mean that their religion did not pay enough attention to their individuality. My students are not selfish. They did not necessarily grow up thinking about religion as a consumer product—something inevitably to be discarded. They simply reached a point where religion did not speak to their experience.

I'm not taking the side of students against religious leaders, just noting that religion has to attend to the individuality in North America's spiritual culture without succumbing to individualism. Maybe we need a new phrase, something like *relational individuality*. We need something that helps people integrate their private life (individual aspirations) and their public life (social responsibility); something that helps people experience the meaning of work (individual aspirations) and allows them to see work's contribution to the common good as an instrument of culture (social responsibility); something that helps people feel uplifted (individual aspiration) and instills a sense of loyalty to particular communities and the whole world (social responsibility). In my circles around Chicago, that something is being called a *spirituality of work*.

My Companions
on the Journey

I t is the very rare person who can make sense of the spiritual life all alone. I am not that person. My vocation came to me in the context of my parents and siblings. It was shaped and nurtured in grammar school and high school by neighbors, relatives, classmates, teachers and parish priests. It was sharpened and critiqued by professors and friends in college. It is sustained by my wife, my children, my extended family, my professional colleagues, and my friends—some of whom date back to high school.

Invest in a support group, I strongly advise my college students. Don't make the spiritual journey without a forum in which to share your struggle for meaning. I've even developed this short list of do's and don'ts for support groups:

- A support group is naturally somewhat informal, but it also must have a rudimentary structure: Maybe a set question to focus conversation, maybe an article from a magazine, whatever.
- A support group must meet regularly, no less than five times a year.
- A support group requires fidelity. There will be many meetings you don't feel like going to and some that you don't get much out of. There will be, however, some meetings where your needs are met because of the fidelity of the others.

- On the other hand, a support group is not a life-long commitment. In fact, most groups plateau after five or six meetings. So if it does not feel right after the first set of meetings, bail out.
- There's no magic to the group's composition regarding gender, occupations or other criteria. All kinds of groups click; all kinds of groups fizzle.
- A group that becomes all socializing is probably worth sustaining, but it is not a support group.

For about twenty-five years I have participated in a weekly Cursillo group. We meet for lunch on Fridays. There are four regulars, all guys: an insurance broker, an investment advisor, a lawyer, and myself. One original member, a realtor, died last year and there is one other, a pastor, who attends infrequently. After some conversation about sports and politics, we answer some fixed questions. We usually don't interrupt to give one another advice. We close with a prayer for any missing group members and then go back to work. Here are the Cursillo questions (paraphrased for people unfamiliar with the program):

- What has been my "piety" this previous week? (This question recognizes that worship and prayer are essential.)
- What has been my "moment closest to Christ" in the previous week? (This is a trick question because it disposes us to look for Christ all week long. In my experience with Cursillo, the question also makes Christ existentially present to me because I am not aware of him in many weekday moments until after the fact when our support group convenes on Friday.)
- What has been my "study" this week? (This question recognizes the intellectual component to the spiritual life. Answers can include any type of article, book, lecture or film.)
- What have been my successes and/or failures this week at home, on the job, and in the community? (This question, which can be

answered in whole or part, attends to the action component of the spiritual life.)

Many Fridays I am tempted to skip our group reunion because I have too many tests to correct or too many calls to make or too tight a deadline on something I am writing. But over the years, my Friday group has been an extremely valuable resource in holding myself accountable to the calling I've been given. My support group doesn't supply specific guidance. Instead, it gives me a forum in which to articulate the meaning embedded in my experience and allows me to hear other men make a story out of their experience.

Over the years, my Friday group has been an extremely valuable resource in holding myself accountable to the calling I've been given.

A support group's effectiveness is destroyed if expectations are unreasonable. A support group cannot solve every problem. It does not exhaust the quest for meaning. It is simply and profoundly a good tool for the long haul.

Another spiritual discipline I practice regularly may sound like *going to lunch with my friends*, but for thirty years I have made a habit of having appointments with interesting people on a regular basis. Meeting new people on a regular basis is a spiritual discipline that fits somewhere between strictly socializing and strictly business.

Last month, for example, I made the following appointments: an afternoon appointment in the office of a college vice-president, lunch with a pastor in a nearby town, a morning appointment with a high-profile lawyer in the Loop, an afternoon appointment with a musician, a noon appointment with a public official in his office, a breakfast appointment with the president of a foundation, a lunch appointment with a professor from another college, a short appointment in the evening with a leader from a local mosque, a morning appointment with a local businessman. That is, I initiated nine appointments last month. Three were with people I had never met; six with people I meet once or twice a year. These nine appointments were in addition to my normal job appointments, though they clearly can and often do benefit my job.

I persistently make these one-on-one relational appointments in order to gain clarity about my vocation. Of course, I don't call someone to say, "Let's get together for my spiritual direction." The ostensible purpose of the meeting is more practical. For example, "I am teaching a new course at the college and need advice" or "My church is starting a homeless shelter and I need your thoughts." The key for me, however, is not an exchange of information. What I really want is to learn what motivates other active people. In doing so, I invariably gain insight into my own striving and struggle.

This spiritual discipline is not a technique, which is why it is difficult to explain. There are probably people who understand its dynamics and its purpose better than I. There are people who conduct relational appointments at a faster clip and take them to more profound depths. I am an amateur, but one who is enriched by meeting with people simply for the sake of a relationship. My habit not only enriches me but also in its own small way helps replenish our society's social capital.

Robert Putnam, in *Bowling Alone* (Simon & Schuster, 2000) and elsewhere, documents a forty-year precipitous decline in all voluntary associations in this country. Churches, clubs, and almost all other organizations are suffering from a lack of new members. When this happens, society suffers too because daily life becomes more callous and less responsive. Reflecting on Putnam's findings, I have concluded that society will not mend by happenstance. Caring people must schedule relational appointments with deliberation and calculation, year after year.

In addition to our families and friends, we need heroes, saints and mentors if we are to follow our vocations. Our modern culture has an abundance of celebrities and a paucity of heroes. Celebrities are easier to deal with. When they stumble we can cynically dismiss them. By settling for celebrities, we accept a perpetual state of disappointment, assured that everyone is less than they appear.

Heroes are more difficult. When they stumble we have to optimistically factor our disappointment into our admiration. Real heroes, mentors and saints are not plastic figures. They are not one-dimensional. They warrant admiration precisely because they are complex characters.

Father Mychal Judge, OFM, who heroically rushed to the burning World Trade Center in order to save lives and comfort the dying, was the first to be buried following the attack on September 11, 2001. Father Judge is an outstanding example of Christian service. But what do we do with Father Judge's homosexuality, his battle with alcoholism, and his occasional unpleasantness?

Dr. Martin Luther King, Jr., only twenty-six years old when he led the Montgomery bus boycott, is rightly regarded as a hero for civil rights. Yet King was an adulterer. He was paternalistic toward women in the movement and had other flaws, personal and public.

It's fun to dish about movie stars, sports figures, and other celebrities because we can smugly disassociate ourselves from them. But we also need heroes, without whom we are more prone to fear and pessimism. Heroes prompt us to choose a career and to stick with it. Heroes allow us to imagine wholeness or holiness. Heroes help us find courage and fortitude. Heroes remind us that being a victim doesn't bestow special wisdom or privileged status.

To have heroes, however, is to wrestle with inconsistencies, to be faithful to the essentials, to process momentary discouragement, and to sustain long-term commitment.

My heroes include some well-known saints such as Paul, the risk-taking organizer; Thomas More, the principled layman; Pope John

XXIII, the pious revolutionary; and Francis of Assisi, the counter-cultural mystic. During the 1960s, I was fortunate to meet some Catholic champions of justice including Cesar Chavez, Dorothy Day, and Robert Kennedy. I am also inspired by pioneering North American Catholics of days gone by, including Charles Carroll, St. Elizabeth Seton, Bishop John Ireland, and Father Isaac Hecker, the founder of the Paulists.

Hecker was a convert to Catholicism, having tried transcendental-ism among other ideas. He was ordained a Redemptorist priest, a religious order founded in Italy. But Hecker wanted to minister in a North American style. He wanted to live in a row house, not a rectory as such. He wanted to preach to Protestants. The Redemptorists eventually kicked him out of their order. Here's part of a sermon Hecker preached in Manhattan in 1863, a quotation that encapsulates my vocation:

> Every age has its own characteristics [and] a type of sanctity peculiar to itself.... Our age [here in the United States] is not an age of martyrdom, nor an age of hermits, nor a monastic age. Although it has its martyrs, its recluses, and its monastic communities, these are not and are not likely to be its prevailing types of Christian perfection. Our age lives in its busy marts, in counting rooms, in workshops, in homes and in the varied relations that form human society. It is into these that sanctity is to be introduced.... Out of the cares, toils, duties, afflictions and responsibilities of daily life are to be built the pillars of sanctity of our age.

I've also consistently sought out mentors, including the priests at my boyhood parish, some of my teachers in college, and more recently the people associated with social action in Chicago. All of my heroes have flaws, which is partially how they inspire me.

Some Other Disciplines

I t is puzzling to me why some young adults invest so much energy and time in their education and yet following graduation never subscribe to a journal or a substantial magazine. Preaching to my students about the importance of reading is futile. So instead, I arrive early for every single class. I sit aside my desk and read. Not the textbook, but a magazine or journal. I then try to refer to the article, if only obliquely, during the class.

An interesting Christian must be constantly reading, particularly literature and biographies, because they instill character and virtue.

Many years ago my high school classmate, Father Jim Callan, suggested I keep a journal. I initially rejected the idea, but later I bought a stenographer's notebook in which to jot my thoughts. I now possess a substantial diary, almost forty volumes.

Human memory is different from a computer that can store and later retrieve intact documents. Human memory is different from a Xerox machine that can make exact copies. Memory is selective, and it retrieves material in altered form. "We store in memory only images of value," writes Patricia Hampl in *I Could Tell You Stories: Sojourns in the Land of Memory* (W.W. Norton, 1999). But, she continues, "the value may be lost over the passage of time."

What makes for value-enriched memory? What mediates between memory and consciousness? It is, I feel, the soul that draws upon memory and brings things to consciousness, wrapping details in color, humor, embellishments and lessons. A well-ordered soul helps a person to discover meaning in life by changing isolated incidents into a body of experience. Without soul, life is at best a series of episodes. The soul takes events and refashions them into a drama, a story, a meaningful existence.

When I started my journal in 1968, I thought its purpose was to preserve exact details, like on a computer disk (although personal computers had yet to be invented). I quickly realized that the deeper truth of my life story emerges only if my soul has free play with details. The memory-soul-consciousness process needs details, but it also needs a plot line and some themes and plenty of literary license. The truth in my life cannot get hung up on chronology. This is not to say that I misrepresent dates on my resume or that I forge personal documents. But in making a story of my life, a couple events from the 1960s, for example, fit better with a dominant theme from the 1970s. Here is Patricia Hampl explaining her approach to writing a memoir:

> My desire was to be accurate. [But that turned out to be] very different from transcription. I am forced to admit that memory is not a warehouse of finished stories, not a gallery of painted pictures. I must admit that I invented.... Memoir must be written because each of us must possess a created version of the past. Created: That is, real in the sense of tangible, made of the stuff of life lived in place and in history. And the downside of any created thing as well: We must live with a version that attaches us to our limitations, to the inevitable subjectivity of our points of view. We must acquiesce to our experience and our gift to transform experience into meaning. You tell me your story, I'll tell you mine.

My Catholic Identity

Over the past twenty-five years, I have taught a course in World Religion each semester at Moraine Valley Community College. It not only brings me in contact with the history and dogma of the major traditions but also into conversation about religion with the very diverse students at our college. My study of world religions and my close association with non-Catholics has, not unexpectedly, provoked a crisis for me. Is it possible, I have had to consider, that non-Catholics have the same access to heaven as other Christians? What do we Catholics mean by *salvation* anyway? If there's some legitimacy to other religious traditions, what's so great about being a Christian?

Father Francis Feeney was my boyhood pastor back in Irondequoit, New York. For some reason he often told me the story of Father Leonard Feeney, SJ, in Boston (no relation to my pastor). Leonard Feeney was a crusader for the literal and extreme position: "There is no salvation outside the Catholic Church." The Vatican condemned this position in 1949 and excommunicated Father Feeney. My pastor, the "other" Father Feeney, provided the punch line: "So I guess now Father Feeney can't be saved."

My pastor's story became embedded in the culture of our little parish and in my own outlook. He didn't delineate its lessons, but I readily concluded that it is one thing to be proud of our Catholicism, but it is very wrong to put down people of other traditions. Later I learned that the Vatican letter, meant to correct the Feeneyites in Boston, spoke of "baptism of desire," noting that such a desire does not have to "be explicit." I also learned that Catholicism fully recognizes all Christian baptisms—except those outside of Trinitarian form. I also heard about "anonymous Christians," people never exposed to Christ but who, in some spiritual way, implicitly desire what Christ offers.

My immediate family and my circle of friends include Protestants, Orthodox Christians, Muslims and Jews. Some are in my circle by happenstance, but several are there more or less *because of* our religious difference. I've discovered that any serious encounter between two or more religions, cultures or families provokes a crisis. But the outcome can be a strengthening of faith, culture, and family life.

> *Under the right conditions, I have found that Catholics who engage in respectful dialogue deepen their own faith and effectively share the truth.*

The ecumenical or interreligious process is not magic. Competent dialogue leaders are a necessary part of the vision. So too are experienced teachers and savvy community organizers. But under the right conditions, I have found that Catholics who engage in respectful dialogue (either in a formal interreligious group or by cooperating with others on civic issues) deepen their own faith and effectively share the truth.

Is there, then, such a thing as one true religion? My conviction is that Jesus is the Way, the Truth and the Life; further, Catholicism gets me closer to the (capital T) Truth. That is not surprising. Catholic is who I am. I could no more stop being Catholic than I could stop being male, Irish-American or handsome (smile).

In understanding my Catholic identity, however, I have been very influenced by another Chicagoan, Father Andrew Greeley, who writes about the Catholic "sacramental" or "analogical" imagination. In his books (I have over twenty-five nonfiction books by Greeley in my office), Greeley uses stories and sociological data to show how Catholics are disposed to the benevolence of God embedded in the ordinariness of life. For Catholics, this is a grace-filled world. God is lurking amid the mundane details of work and family life. God is praised inside the church building through the liturgy (from a Greek word meaning *the work of the people*) as well as outside the church build-ing through the liturgy of the workaday world. Because they imagine God as proximate and loving, Catholics are quite comfortable with all kinds of pictures, statues and religious objects, including multitudinous depictions of our Blessed Lady, the primary feminine metaphor for God.

The Catholic outlook is optimistic about the world around us. This disposition, Greeley stresses, isn't better or worse than an outlook more wary of the world, more attuned to sinfulness. But the Catholic appro-priation of Christianity is certainly different. And the Catholic way is better for me. It fits my Irish-American temperament. It supports my fascination with ethnicity and urban neighborhoods. It corresponds with my involvements in community organizations and labor issues. It helps me appreciate the religious dimension of my job, my marriage, and my parenting. It gives an added, sacramental dimension to some of my favorite activities: going to lunch with a friend, telling stories at a party, visiting the elderly, sharing half a bottle of wine with my spouse. It's great to be a Christian and even greater for me to be a Catholic!

Being Catholic is not an option for me. It is not a preference, some-thing I choose. I am not doing the church a favor by being a member. My Catholic Christianity is a gift. Nothing will cause me to return that gift.

The word *church* carries several meanings. Adjectives can be used to distinguish one sense of church from another: the parish church, the mystical church, the institutional Church, and more. The temptation to replace the word *church* with another noun, however, must be resisted. *Church* is a powerful word precisely because it has layers of meaning. Ultimately, I've had to submit to the power of the church.

I love the church…and the Church. No stupid pronouncement from a Vatican department, no scandalous behavior by a Church leader, no boring homily or pointless parish meeting can cause me to abandon it. People who leave over such things don't understand sin or forgiveness. And they do not understand what it means to love an institution.

Of course, I've shopped around for vibrant worship. Of course, I've dissented from certain interpretations of rules or political positions taken by the hierarchy. Of course, I'm deeply embarrassed by the malfeasance of our bishops. I certainly respect people who change denominations in protest or to accommodate a spouse or friend. But those of us who believe in the church can never truly leave it.

My Christian vocation is not something I requested. It comes with a burden, especially during these days when so many bishops and other Church leaders are so attached to social standing and lacking in courage. It is oftentimes hard to proclaim my gratitude for it.

But my Catholicism is a great gift. I hope my children—and their children and their children's children—will feel the same, for the worst kind of unemployment is to be without a vocation.